The Possibility of Reddish Green

Wittgenstein Outside Philosophy

Also by David Rothenberg

Is It Painful to Think?

Hand's End

Blue Cliff Record

Sudden Music

Always the Mountains

Why Birds Sing

Thousand Mile Song

Survival of the Beautiful

Bug Music

Nightingales in Berlin

The Possibility of Reddish Green

Wittgenstein Outside Philosophy

David Rothenberg

Terra Nova Press
NEWARK   CALLICOON   MATSALU

2020

© 2020 by David Rothenberg
ISBN: 978-1-949597-07-3
Library of Congress Control Number: 2020932920
All rights reserved.

published by:

Terra Nova Press
NEWARK   CALLICOON   MATSALU

Editor-in-Chief: Evan Eisenberg
Designer: Martin Pedanik
Proofreader: Tyran Grillo
Cover Art: Bernhard Wöstheinrich
set in Minion, Gotham, Century and Source Sans
printed by Tallinn Book Printers, Tallinn Estonia

1 2 3 4 5 6 7 8 9 10
www.terranovapress.com

Distributed by the MIT Press, Cambridge, Massachusetts
and London, England

In a world of universal poverty
The philosophers alone will be fat
Against the autumn winds
In an autumn that will be perpetual.

—Wallace Stevens[1]

Preface and Explanation of Form

Ludwig Wittgenstein may have been a philosopher, but philosophers have always gotten the guy dead wrong. They claim he is the founder of two competing schools of thought. In essence, though, he is a poet, an aphorist, and an inspiration to thousands the world over: artists, writers, miscreants, dreamers, searchers, in other words: could be anybody. This is what philosophers dream of: changing people's minds just a little bit by explaining the world a slightly different way.

So, naively, I decided I would write something aphoristic and impelled by Wittgenstein's exemplary and extreme life. It's thirty years since I first thought of doing this, and so much in the world has changed, while so much has not changed. I tried to publish this book many times and it always almost came out before it was shot down by philosophers knowing far more than I who said I was disrespectful, ignorant, and missing the point.

Those things may be true, but after so many years I cannot shake the feeling that it is time to let the reader judge.

Some say art should become more like philosophy; I think philosophy should become more like art. And I maintain that's what Wittgenstein was thinking, too.

Wittgenstein wrote his insights down in fragments, the tweets of his day, sometimes aphorisms, sometimes disconnected paragraphs, pieces of barely envisioned works he knew he could never complete. He published only one work during his lifetime, *Tractatus Logico-Philosophicus*, a slim, tightly orchestrated volume of logically separated sentences that argues either that the world is nothing but a collection of facts, or else that words cannot describe what is most important about life. Wittgenstein is both precise and ambiguous, meticulously poetic, solid but transparent, like a cube of slowly melting black ice.

His philosophical self-criticism and inner suffering may be difficult to comprehend in any organized fashion, but it is easy to be inspired by pieces of his questioning. Perhaps this is all we should expect from philosophy—after all, which of the grand systems of thought in the discipline's history can be said to be *correct*? None of them. The process of inventing such a system is ambitious, possibly lucid, often impressive. But rarely do we congratulate a philosopher for being right.

Philosophy deals with the "kind of questions that can be answered in no other way," read the old department brochure from Harvard when I was an undergraduate there in the 1980s. Since then my own experience has suggested to me that philosophy deals with the kind of questions that can only be answered by other questions, or the kind of questions one must stop pursuing in order to answer them.

I mean: to make sense of the rich disturbances in the flow of human thought and action that philosophy engenders, it may be necessary to turn away from it, or to approach one's unease from a radically different tack. At the end of his only nonposthumous book, the *Tractatus*, Wittgenstein tells us, famously, that if we understand what he is driving at, we will not need the book anymore, we will not need the method. We will have reached the plane which the ladder of propositions has allowed us to climb up to, and we may kick it aside because it is impossible to retrace one's steps, anyway.

Writers and artists outside the official community of philosophers refer more often to W than to any other philosopher of the last century. He has inspired all kinds of thoughtful people, challenging them to push their own disparate visions further in a sober but inquisitive, open manner.

Both his life and ideas have captured mass intellectual attention. He came to his vocation by drive and by default. He tried everything else to avoid doing philosophy, but there was simply nothing else he could do. He continually advised his students to leave the field, to do something in the "real" world. He gave an inherited fortune away and lived in as spartan a way as he could. His life was so exemplary that no one else could possibly duplicate it. Who would want to? Would anyone else have responded to those times and that legacy in the same way?

And so Wittgenstein becomes an exemplar of one sober way to react to the doubt of our time, while at the same time offering a relentless answer: a poetic kind of questioning, a severe but enveloping openness to new traces of logic and previously invisible connections between different kinds of thought, different styles of intellectual life.

W can at times seem a weird and depressing sort of fellow, but his vision is anything but bleak. He was fascinated by the odd and latent links between the way we act in the world and how we try to explain it. The puzzle that is philosophy would never loosen its hold on him—his best attempts at breaking free come in the form of brief and pithy poetic insights, beautiful islands of language impossible to reduce to the rubric of logic.

This is why Wittgenstein advocates poetic as much as analytic philosophy. Writers turn their attention on him as a character to try to break through the puzzle: astonishingly, there are at least six novels in which he is a major character. The serial re-invention of a philosopher's life is worthy of attention, but we are taught that fiction is more entertaining than philosophy. By delving into these works, along with the films and artworks that have been produced around him, I aim to show that serious philosophy is contained in these approaches, that Wittgenstein requires many ways of inquiry to become more than a symbol of himself and his own malaise.

His ideas and thought style are a challenge for the future of philosophy. They open up its borders, allow more of us to join in the chase. It is no accident that Wittgenstein has touched a chord in the culture of the world today. He points a way that philosophy can be relevant, can remain alive. This book is meant to show aspects of this relevance that have been previously overlooked by the profession of philosophy. It is not so much a study of Wittgenstein as a case for the influence of philosophy outside its own borders.

There is more to response than argument; there is more to poetry than the surprise of images. Logic walks not the fence but the ridge between watersheds of human inquiry. From the top of the range, the whole world can be seen. If you remember all shoulders of the mountain you will be able to ascend any one of the ridges whenever you want.

I:

Cloudbuilding

He was someone who could not quite do what he would like to do. (Or at least that's what he said.)

Was it the world that stood in his way—that troublesome collection of facts, or silent emotions? That century of tumult and exploded dreams, a wonderful and terrible time. The time from which logic has chiseled words away to reveal it as an empty, quiet space.

Wittgenstein wanted to turn philosophy into poetry, yet perhaps they have two disparate aims. One wants to imagine language can be precise enough to explain away the subtlety of things with the crystal of logic; the other senses that logic is not as pure as the spaces between words, those truths that words evoke by not believing in the attunement of clarity.

Poetry and philosophy both seem to require more patience than this world right now wants to allow—the phalanx of images, the upset of change, the transformations far beyond any one person's control. These two responses to the world ask for too much clarity to be heard above the loudness we see all around us, flashing, buzzing in electrified and digitized color, light, and sound. Yet they hide beneath the explosion of surfaces. The poetic encapsulates the fragments which are all we are expected to understand. The philosophic takes refuge in recurring questions when any answer seems inadequate or just too hard.

Wittgenstein told other philosophers to leave the field, to do something useful, to work with their hands, to administer care to the sick and the dying. He tried these things himself, and still he could not keep from the abstract. (A man without compromise.) Using utmost care in what he felt he could say, he skirted around the most important things because he lacked the language to speak of them. Ethics, beauty, how to live in the most troubled of times. Above all else, Wittgenstein cared about these things. Yet he did not feel comfortable speaking of them. Talking around them was all he could do, telling people to act as one should act, not as one feels content to act when the ideal is too stringent for the actuality.

All those who remain attracted to his words and deeds are equally bound inextricably to the abstract. We spend so much of our time reaching for thin air, and are either astonished or disheartened by how thick it is.

Most philosophers tend to imagine that Wittgenstein makes conventional sense, that his aphorisms hold onto a system of thought, one that can be scrutinized as such. If this is how he survives, then, like all his predecessors, his system will be proven incorrect. Kant, Hegel, Spinoza, Aristotle. They all tried to explain too much. Sure, they changed their societies, their times—but in claiming completeness for their systems, they were all wrong.

Wittgenstein had a system, then he threw it away. Nothing he wrote after that felt ready for publication, ready to let loose on the world. So many notebooks: Blue, Brown. Psychology, Mathematics. Worldviews insinuated out of scraps of paper. So many clues, on so many shards. Left in boxes, held together by paper clips. These circumstances should not be forgotten. His executors brushed chaos into order.

Others say: it is because of these small fragments that Wittgenstein looms so large. Many of us feel best with just a piece of a philosophy. A fortune inside a cookie to bite into. A sweet coating of method, a few provocative lines inside. One or two philosophical questions is enough to perplex a whole lifetime.

So Wittgenstein reaches outside his field in the form of fragments.

And this is the century of the fragment, the decade of the Tweet, when the long form cannot hold. To the left and to the right, tattered shreds of culture blow in the wind. Wittgenstein worked hard, but he did not pull these insights altogether into any one presentable whole. There was no way he could be finally satisfied.

No wonder philosophers have no patience with his method. He believed in turning his writing into poetry, though he never spoke much of poetry. He seemed to be impressed by the power of words left surrounded by space. When held up like that for all to see, they develop a kind of resonance that logic only impairs.

Thought held aloft by the buoyancy of the margin and the break.

"You can't *build* clouds. And that's why the future you *dream* of never comes true."[2] That line shows deeply the place between poetry and philosophy. We can watch the clouds and imagine what objects they may resemble. They're up there all right. But just when we think we have named them for what they are, they have changed. I am already becoming false by trying to surround that cloud of an idea with any semblance of explanation.

Wittgenstein is at his best, the critic in me wants to say, when he is *between* poetry and philosophy. As he creates his own genre, a delicate way to write that survived his stark century. He is at his worst when he tries to shut down emotion—to reduce all to cold facts.

It happens every time. In so many classrooms, all over the world. Some student is bound to get into trouble. He sifts all through Wittgenstein, and then tries to *be* Wittgenstein. You've seen them before, with that penetrating, hollow gaze. Not the wounded, caged hunger of a Kafka, no, something more chilling, impossible to lie to, like an honest priest needing to flee the faith to which he belongs upon discovering a flaw in its underpinning. He is saying with the eyes: tell the truth. Take your time. The student may not just reflect this look. He may also try to learn by example. To write something not about W, but in the style of W. The professor rolls her eyes.

I am attracted to these remarks of W's that are not considered to be at the core of his thought, but at the edges. I suspect it is also these notations that have inspired those outside of philosophy to consider the thorny presence of this philosopher in the midst of their century. He has asked for the impossible, and the necessary: not philosophy of poetry, but poetry in philosophy—configurations of words that change the way we see the world.

It's not only language that's the limit of his world, to quote his most famous phrase. A style of writing only extends so far. "I cannot write verse," complains this would-be poetic philosopher. So then, he knew none of this was poetry. And why not? The words 'poetry' and 'philosophy' each scare different sorts of people away.

I think of my friend Chris B living in a Cambridge basement, sheltered in the dark away from the clouds. He is up all night, writing with colored crayons in huge clothbound folios. Copying each phrase out of Wittgenstein's work On Certainty, *adding his own notes in other colors as he goes. Is this not philosophy most alive, most direct, turning away from the light and the condensation in the air? Is this not the obsession essential for the quest at its core? He is too serious, and then works too hard. His professors disagree so much with his method that they fail him out of all the philosophy courses. He leaves the university and takes up babysitting. Finds another college, and majors in the study of children. Then his obsession with logic leads him into computing, then toward the construction of graphics programs in education. Programming now, he is back to his questions: When the machine does what it is told, is it certain? Leaving philosophy, explaining through devices to the next generation. Has he done with the questions what Ludwig advised? Look into his eyes to decide if he cares.*

I have only fragments to read, and only a portion of these fragments matters at all to me. Surrounded by the barrage of information, the structure is easy to miss.

"In the ticket offices of English railway stations after World War Two, this admonishment: 'Is your journey really necessary?'"[3] Save fuel, stay at home. Wittgenstein wanted anyone who found themselves puzzling over a philosophical question to ask this very question. If you have nowhere to go, what can you hope to discover? He wants someone to tell him if there is any reason to think so much about all these strange, unanswerable things.

How can he be sure he hasn't written poetry? It does not read like philosophy. Schiller said that the poetic mood is that deep receptivity when one's thoughts are as vivid as nature itself. Expressing those thoughts is something else again.

Coming closer to a joke, we learn from W the philosopher's salute: "Take your time!" Completing a philosophy might take more than one lifetime—that's why they're never done. The most that can be said for any great system is that it is right on the mark once in a while, like a clock that is broken. As a whole it is bound to be corrupt, because no system absolves us of the need for every other system. At an instant it may just explain what seems impossible to fathom. Poetry celebrates such moments. Philosophies want to offer at least a possible reason for why they are there at all.

The inscrutability of a phrase suggests the accidental nature of signs and what they stand for. But it is the fortuitous mesh of sound and guess that we admire at a distance, if only for strangeness and the possibility for so many unknowns that still make sense, to someone, somewhere.

Xarxa, the word for *map* in Catalan—letters forced together like a cloud. When spoken it sounds like it's come from behind the mist. There is nothing that can be built all out of words except clouds. Their meanings evaporate as soon as we have agreed upon them.

The possibility; the possibility of a betweenspace that at first can't be seen. A hue between colors that cannot be mixed, a taste between foods that do not blend, a compound of chemicals that flee each other's touch. The blend of the unblendable is the sound our throats cannot produce, the nature that can only be imagined to exist, the word caught somewhere betwixt the mind and the voice, an unpronounceable diagram of the world.

"Ambition is the death of thought." The old Norwegian folk wisdom of the Janteloven states that we should not believe we can accomplish anything, we should not believe we have anything to teach, we should not believe that our quest for learning will get us anywhere. This stern set of commandments enumerated by Danish writer Axel Sandemose was meant to outline a society that believed people should be kept in their place.

Philosophy is supposed to survive only in an atmosphere of austerity. We are not supposed to judge it by what we think we can get from it.

At my college reunion I meet the man who has made the most money since leaving school. On his nametag he lists his profession as 'arbitrageur.' "Philosophy," he muses, nursing a wineglass, "now there's where you find the best questions. No doubt about it. But you never get the answers. On Wall Street, I get my answers every day. At 4:00 pm. Nice talking to you."

Patience is the prerequisite for the writing of this book. I am here first to report a phenomenon, a growing sense that philosophy is seeping out into society in ways that are not usually tracked. Yet I find myself often lacking in patience. The air seems too thin, too thick, too dry, too moist, proverbially not right. The net of paths ending at my door seems destined to remain tangled, emanating out, always going somewhere else. It is difficult to close the book, let alone to open it.

I do not think of Wittgenstein as necessarily patient. But like the Buddha, he did take his time. He was driven, driven into philosophy and out of it. This century could not hold him. It was not the place where he wanted to be. So he changed his time by renouncing the life that had been given him. (As D.T. Suzuki said to John Cage: "In philosophy, no one wins": that weight of the war without answers.) Three of the five brothers Wittgenstein killed themselves. Ludwig chose instead to sever himself absolutely from his fortune. Having money could have been a privilege that might have isolated him from honesty. His quest was too solitary, he wanted to delve beyond the material world. It was philosophy that saved him from the family curse.

A Marxist might say, "You've got to be rich to think like that."

I want to believe there is a reason for the more mature Wittgenstein to spread things out inexactly, believing the strength in a paragraph to depend somewhat on its separation from all others. He would not have connected it further, even if granted more time. He wanted it this way.

He prophesied a poetry where the space surrounding the poem marks the insight as a poem. It is not only the expression but the form of the expression that contains the art of it. Today we have art moving towards philosophy, requiring included explanations to be appreciated. At the same time we find philosophy wanting to be art, depending more on enigma than argument to make its point.

This is the logic of the betweenspaces of things. These are the words that tell you you don't need them when you're through. At the top of the ladder you will find no need to ever go down. If the words got you up there, throw them away. (*Of what we cannot speak, thereupon we must remain silent*—another of his famous lines.) The quality of this silence will be illuminating. It may contain ways to make ourselves known and believed without the ice of words.

Philosophy withers away when it becomes a specialty only concerned with itself. It should not forget its original purpose: to ask the largest questions about what it means to be alive, what it means to be a human being, what it means to be a being who needs to articulate a purpose to survive.

If you are a philosopher you may fault me for taking Wittgenstein's words out of context. And yet I am most interested in those who take him out of context. (Not that he ever told us his context—still the underlying whisper: *no concessions.*) To do this to a thinker so obsessed with context, so intrigued with the idea that our communication is like a game dependent upon the tacit acceptance of rules— this is near to blasphemy. But who is his public? His audience of pupils he urged to leave the field? The would-be disciples who imagine his ideas to form a system? Those who admire his life and his refusal to compromise his feelings or his ideas? Try: anyone who finds themselves inspired by even one word he has written. A writer never chooses her audience. People find the words and make of them what they will.

There is the dilemma of Kafka instructing his best friend Max Brod to destroy all of his manuscripts upon the writer's death. Instead, the good friend made them available to the rest of the world, so that they emerge as anthems of our century. I asked a whole class of students about this, and nearly all of them replied that Max betrayed his friend by letting the work out into the public domain. I could not agree with them: Do not the words belong to whoever finds them, detaching them thus from the context of their author? We contribute to a culture by letting our words *go.* It is only in our lives that we must be responsible.

"All that we see could also be otherwise. *All that we describe at all could also be otherwise.*"[4] This is what one must believe to even consider philosophy. That things are seldom what they seem. That skim milk may masquerade as cream. Beginning with doubt, we imagine everything may fit together another way. It does not matter how sure we are about the other way. People will still have to want to work to change their way of seeing things. What's in it for them? A new worldview is nothing but trouble. The connection between new ways of thinking and new acts is not always direct. They have a subtle influence on each other.

Never mind if *the point is to change it*, the world still may look different after philosophy. Today art and philosophy are pushed against each other into the arena of the question. I want to know exactly where it is that Wittgenstein finds he fails to write poetry. After him, poetry has become more like him. By setting space between question and answer, he leaves from logic and arrives near art:

> How can man be happy at all, since he cannot ward off the misery of this world?

> Through the life of knowledge.[5]

That first question is an art-stopping question, a collapse into hopelessness. Knowledge is only a half-serious answer here. Wittgenstein's answer could just as well lie in the space above the sentence.

He always surrounds his words with space, above and below each statement or aphorism. That's where our own words might have space to fit in.

On the other hand, Ludwig may simply doubt himself, or else be having us on: "Only remember that the spirit of the snake, of the lion, is *your* spirit. For it is only from yourself that you are acquainted with spirit at all." A sensual grasp at the animal world, a recognition of the power of soul, or else simply a beautiful image.

Why this age-old confounding of philosophy and litera-ture anyway? The majority of the great systems of thought are terribly written, awfully turgid. Is this the consequence of language being stretched into places where it does not want to go?

The standard answer is that philosophy is not composed of words, but of ideas or at least questions that lie beyond the limits of words. The words are vehicles to take us to a place where they then become redundant, unnecessary, hindrances toward holding on to the truth. That's why when you have understood the *Tractatus*, you may cast it away, for its ladder of propositions will no longer be of use to you. (Is this why there are so many used copies for sale in the basement bookstores of universities worldwide?)

Perhaps I am the one not taking my subject seriously.

To take the subject seriously does not always mean to de-rive his logic from his words. In the spaces between the words may come the meaning. In those remaining empty spaces on the map, our culture finds its last remaining truths.

Writers of fiction have taken Wittgenstein very seriously, though they may dispute his two divergent famous points, that the world is composed of facts, or that we use language as if it were a game, where the rules must be known and internalized before a message is sent and received. Most though not all games are supposed to be fun. And joy in life can only partially be explained.

Artists have played with Wittgenstein, they have framed his message in new contexts, mixing inspiration from aspects of his life, aspects of his ideas, and aspects of the way he presents those ideas. I do not so much want to analyze the way these artists have dealt with the inspiration of their subject as write a response in the style of the subject himself. He was not a scholar, but a thinker. In its aspiration toward poetry, his approach to analysis does not reduce its object of inquiry. He bounced off his surroundings to incidentally define our time.

The classic philosopher's mistake is to imagine that thinking alone can offer a system of the world. In their systems the greatest thinkers have failed, yet in moments of insight they have approached the truth. W's writing is composed of those moments. The system is up to us to imagine. And we can imagine it only if we recognize that it cannot exist, not in any conventional sense. The truth lies only in relationships—from fragment to fragment, observation to equation.

Wittgenstein writes a new kind of book. One that will be impossible to categorize, that will not fit neatly on any one shelf. There are still new kinds of books to be written, a century later. The possible orders of words already admit the realm of the new. One trajectory cannot encompass all the pathways of thoughts going through us, reflecting this material back to us, over all the many years.

II:

Investigate

part 1, Numbered

I read Wittgenstein's *Philosophical Investigations,* and pause only when inspired. This seems to be the most natural method for those who want to find our own order among the fragments. We look for something that supports the path our mind is taking. We use the book to push further along this path.

Choose the color or the shape. Blue here now. A circle. A cloud. For a painter, he worried: "It's hard to get the blue of this sky"[6] How do we know what is blue and what is not? (It was the last color to be named, old languages don't have it—think of the Homer's "wine-dark sea.") Calling attention to the roots of the world.

"Something red can be destroyed, but red cannot be destroyed."[7] Teaching by example that a color is not a thing. And the positive among us ask: Then, can red be created? Or was it always there? Is it seen, named, part of the spectrum as some unity—only as the result of human physiology? The bright cardinals see each other differently as they flit from the trees onto the snow, the contrast always different each time one of us cares to notice. The flag is torn to tatters by the storm, no one cares to say the red disappears. If we bleach it in the wash, then the red disappears. Or the drops in the eye get the red out. But red remains all along. Except—are there not human cultures with no need to see it, with no word for the color 'red'?

And Wittgenstein has written differently about red than he has of blue. Blue is the sky, a fond memory one should try to paint. Red is a sadness, it washes away, fading with the entropy of time. And still it is there. Blue can't be remembered, though we desperately try..

What is the *shape* of blue, or the shape of red? How to present them in their standard forms? There is no way to catalog them, no method to put them away, yet that does not appear to lessen their significance.

It is not the same to know and to say these, and other, things. W's almost haiku:

> how many feet high Mont Blanc is—
> how the word 'game' is used—
> how a clarinet sounds.[8]

These lines proceed from fact, through convention, into the indescribable. *I have played it for years, but I cannot explain how a clarinet sounds.* The name of the instrument suggests clarity. There is a woodiness in its precision. I could mention the odd-only overtone structure, and clarify the tone that way. It always sounds different each time and place, yet always the experienced ear can tell this is a clarinet. Wittgenstein too played the clarinet; Brahms, I hear, was his favorite. Language is not prepared to speak away music—that is not how the game of words is played.

"A *picture* held us captive. And we could not get outside it, because it lay in our language and language seemed to repeat it to us inexorably."[9] W's remorse again—he was trapped for years by the picture of the picture theory of language, thrumming in him without pause, that imagistic exactitude of how words were supposed to work as logic. He writes this sentence long after he has given up this ghost, but is he or anyone outside it even now? We approach our world with a whole vision, or smaller images in smaller frames, seeing just what we want or are able to see. We have *colored* our perception by the lenses we choose. It's up to each one of us to discover warmth around this cold, hard fact.

I once knew a man who began a hundred-page poem with the image of a picture holding us captive. He lived into the struggle to free himself from the picture, and ended only more convinced of the invincibility of the frame and the direction that demands the image. He is still caught, he knows just one way to see. That work cannot, of course, be finished.

Someone leads you along, and you are guided.[10] And it is enough to list the many ways this phrase is turned to see that it does not permit exact definition. You are tugged reluctantly by the hand. Your partner leads you in the dance. You are taken for a walk, and do not worry where you go. Being led absolves you of responsibility. (Or does it?—The need to follow and still be yourself.)

When the text stops pointing out a route through its lines and paragraphs, you must find your own path. This is an interactive medium, these lines on the page. There have always been implicit instructions in the very form of the book; it has always been possible to flip through the pages, or tear something out to preserve or discard. Then to xerox or scan, no memory needed. You may file them away, for information seems free. There is no more value put on memory, as the space needed for filing shrinks. In my palm is a silicon repository for twenty-five encyclopedias. It has been made out of sand. The brain stays the same. Even if we imagine it will live eternally in some new kind of cloud.

"When I follow the rule, I do not choose. I follow the rule *blindly*."[11] When doing so, I cannot help myself. I am among the rules, doing what I was never told to do, only what I know. Act according to plan, with those rules straight and narrow, extending like tracks to the horizon, forever, where they will never meet. That's how they work without fail.

Wittgenstein heard also the paradox in the preponderance of modal music through time. This is music without the internalized ii-V-I conclusions of the baroque and classical styles, but with the stranger, more ambiguous endings of medieval and Gregorian chant. Heard from within the classical tradition, these early meandering melodies are inconclusive. They move with less clarity. They have their own, unfamiliar rules. "What happens when we learn to *feel* the end of a church mode as an ending?"[12] He is asking: what happens when we understand a foreign music, a sound world with its own logic.

The same shift inside I remember from studying the music of Tibet many years ago.[13] At first, it all sounds the same: inconclusive, distant. When it begins to make sense, one could say we have learned its rules. It is a music where only a few tones in the scale are allowed; each tiny variation contains a wealth of significance. Just when you think you know what's supposed to happen, a surprise is written in. Why? It cannot be explained. But it is something else again to *feel* its correctness. When the rules actually matter to us we forget they exist. We act without explanation, hear something and smile without knowing why.

Later W is flummoxed by an inability to describe the smell of coffee.[14] Not only a picture, but it is the picture of words that holds this man prisoner. They are nothing, these marks on the page, and they grow into obsolescence as each day brings a vaster panoply of images, moving faster, exponentially faster as the culture moves on. Still, some of us hold on to words because they require such focus, such shutting down, such simplicity in the face of the complicated. Smells embrace armloads of memory, coffee serves a purpose and no one can name it. He wants to believe in what he's doing, reading it over while sipping the morning brew. "These notes say something glorious. But I do not know what."[15] We all would like to enjoy W's sense of confidence.

The philosopher wants to believe in what he has written, but he is afraid of words. Of their power. Of their wildness. The *senselessness* of their rules. To be exact and to still let loose, this is the goal of the wildest of philosophies: to find a precision that unfolds, and does not shut down. That is a crystal wisdom to which philosophy might aspire.

Philosophy is the asking of the right questions. Literature is the most creative and evocative answers possible in words. W is alone, he is longing, he is living, remembering, forgetting, and he feels he understands none of it. He is troubled to no end, still lost in wonder at why things work. He, like so many philosophers, does not really want the answer to his questions. They must simply be asked in the most noble, exact, and detached way.

The difference with Wittgenstein is that he *admits* that he must grope for a possible poetry as he does this. The posing of the questions themselves demands elegance. Reiteration. The thrum of longing and loss. Name a person and you aim at the person. "When he meant him, he aimed at him. But how does someone do that when he calls the other person's face to mind? I mean, how does he call *him* to mind? *How does he call him?*"[16]

Who? Anyone.

We can imagine these numbered thoughts to evoke or outline a system. Or we can take them as the pointers toward poetry that they are. Above all, W does not want you to be like him. Leave philosophy, do something useful, escape from the luxury of idle questioning into the urgency of our final time. There will be no disciples of this philosophy, only those inspired to weave it inside and out of themselves. Find your own possibilities.

Following this logic, we are all alone. In such loneliness comes the shadow of the true.

part 2, This is how it takes us in

Part II of the *Investigations* presents a different, looser kind of fragment. These are now considered pieces of another book.[17] The numbered system breaks down, as if it all were a sham. The rigor collapses, and the notes pour out. It's too much to think about, these unanswerable questions, these postures of situations that seem impossible. Are we to quantify these writings just because they shun convention? Or respond only to those that resonate with our moods, or enhance our own creative or explanatory urges?

W admits that animals may display emotions, but he does not think they can hope. He wonders if only those who *talk* can hope. "The manifestations of hope are modifications of this complicated form of life."[18]

Nicholas Mosley wrote an epic novel entitled *Hopeful Monsters*, probably inspired by this passage, about a young couple in love, but torn apart by the cataclysms of the first half of the twentieth century. They meet periodically, he from England and she from Germany, in the expected scenes through the turbulence of these times. Their relationship is defined by absence from each other, they continue to hope for better times when they might be able to be together. When these times come, they find they do not need each other in person as much as they needed the other as an audience for a letter. Finding each other, they know they are meant for each other, but there is no need to hope anymore. They stay together, but a certain coolness sets in between them.

Who are the hopeful monsters? We who survived the twentieth century are, awful in our cruelty, negligence, and the ability to destroy. So we need to reiterate the reason for humanity to continue on into the next century. Because we alone are able to hope, we must. Max and Eleanor live happily but *calmly* ever after. They have already been through the most exciting times in their lives—when in their anguish they came to know hope.

Words carry with them an atmosphere, a *corona of ways* they might be used.[19] Each of us sees the aura differently, depending what we know. On whether we have perused the dictionary, or listened instead to everyone around us. When we speak, we hope others hear the words as we do. Often they do not. Communication is stymied. We offer to explain, but it is not just the word but a way of life that is challenged—so off once more into silence. Or the effort to free words from their meanings and search instead for sense in sound, appearance, or design. Let communication be the message that comes through in spite of logic, beyond the flippancy of rule.

Synæsthesia. Try to feel 'if' and 'but' as the same.[20] If words are to be felt, their logical function is not the arbiter of their truth. I'll say the feeling of 'if' sets up the next phrase to complete: it's an inhale waiting for an ex-, a premise worth nothing without its conclusion. *Then* I am ready for the answer, and it should depend on the first idea.
'

But' adds a qualifying idea that renders the first statement more ambiguous. If I feel these things as the same I have a sense of language not based on logic. Perhaps another language with its own peculiarities. But once considered, this possibility cannot be forgotten: this tearing of the reasons for words, even small ones, apart. 'If' is almost the opposite of 'but,' but not quite. If it were so, then our language would be more logical than present human uncertainty allows.

John Cage read *Finnegans Wake* many times throughout his life. Never was he content to read, he wanted to revise. He took his favorite parts, moved them around, blended them with quotes from Wittgenstein, Thoreau, McLuhan, and the morning news. By casting the *I Ching* he assembled all these fragments together, according to poetic computations he invented. That was one way to form a seamless whole. And if you listened, you would move toward the sounds of the words, not their logical places.

Cage once told me he never understood the meaning of Wittgenstein's writings, though he was touched by the words themselves, and the way they were used.[21] As Wittgenstein himself responded to music, saying that "a passage gives us quite a special feeling…I sing it with a quite particular expression," inseparable from the passage. Feeling and music intertwined. Feeling and philosophy inextricable from each other. Resonance within to the passages of word or sound. You do not need to know the mechanics of music to appreciate it. Could it be the same with philosophy?

Not to write philosophy as song or symphony, but to *hear* it as such. You repeat the chorus in your head when alone. Maybe you've got it on headphones. Or the symphony was vast, thundering from far away as you sat in the back row at Symphony Hall, and you strive now to remember its impact or its structure. The system always fails, but the art in a moment may touch you, maybe you alone, despite all the barriers, all the distractions. Perhaps no one else understood it but you.

Music to the mind: the text is only a score. The rest is up to you. Though you may pursue it in silence, its sound should be imagined along with its sense. It is not enough to see the marks; their life—if they are alive—is in their music. Knowledge begins with finding your voice.

W has implored you to throw the page away once you are done, but that may be too rash. You can't forget what a book does to you, however disturbing. The effect of the work can't be burned, shelved, or given away.

The picture already points to a particular use. "This is how it takes us in."[22] This way of writing, this planned incompleteness with space for reverie. There are holes in our logic, there are empty spots on the map. Once inside this dream, it is hard to imagine closure again. There are just too many stories. In uncertainty you may find sadness or relief, but responsibility is more important than ever. Direction cannot be forsaken in a time of possibility. Take a stand.

The grasp of recognition: suddenly realizing that the person you see before you is a friend you have not seen in many years.[23] A cold sudden way of describing the warm embracing of an unknown friend. Wondering what is going on, how the unknown face becomes the known, searching just for that point where seeing becomes memory.

I have remembered people and then miraculously conjured them into view, as they materialize out of nowhere in front of me. Or gazed at ranges of mountains to discover memories hidden there, in the land, synapses of climbs and trips into the backcountry that my mind has forgotten but the land retains. How many questions can we ask of what we recall?

Wittgenstein's truth table made the science of computing possible. Were he to have written his notations on a computer, as most of us write today, they would be ripe for reshuffling, independence, and brevity, liberated from the linearity of the book. Each idea might suggest many pathways to the next, journeys of cross reference, logic, and allusion to push one thought to the next. And yet the fixity of the book survives—even as an arsenal of questions.

Yes, the crispness of autumn leaves is there. But also the coldness of a steel-girdered office tower. It is empty, troubling, and does not always make me happy to look at things in this step-by-step, reflective way. I'm aiming for a kind of sentence, but I am reminded of the possibility that the way W writes may be more interesting than what he has said. He is, remember, pointing to what cannot be said. Or asking us to say it all a new way. It is up to us to find that way. And we may each take up his challenge differently.

part 3: *Those who have responded*

The coolness is no answer, but a call to arms. What philosophy is poetic, what poesy addresses the philosophical? These fragments suggest situations, and writers have taken off from these to add to Wittgenstein what he does not offer himself. Warmth. Joy. Humor. Belief. Acceptance of society and what it can and cannot do.

Of course, he does have those phrases that suggest he, too, cared about these things. His last words upon his deathbed: "Tell them I had a happy life." Most unexpected, therefore right? A phrase somewhere else: "It would be possible to compose a philosophical work that consisted entirely of jokes." A very dry kind of humor indeed. Statements also of care, and of love, struck out from margin to margin by the literary executors, analysis freaks afraid of emotion and of W's own homosexual anxiety, with feelings either consummated or only trouble.

I do not want to write about these W–inspired works, or even summarize their plots for you. Yet somehow they have cataloged themselves around me, demanding attention. They mean something. They are an anomaly, a whole series of works about one philosopher no one is sure they understand. Captivated by life, his thought, or his way of expression, they suggest roads not taken, happenings never recorded. I feel compelled to read all these things: anything that takes up Wittgenstein's wager, the dream that makes philosophy real by turning it outside itself. They still believe in the significance of abstract thought in an increasingly material culture. Let's find out what they say.

III:

W, Serial Killer

Wittgenstein loved to catch a flick after a lecture. Down to the cinema in Cambridge: hopefully a fast-moving crime story is playing. Getting lost in the plot, that's the thing. The logic, the resolution, probably. The whole thing as metaphor, a story *standing* for something other than itself. Or at the very least, an escape from the *muddle* of philosophy.

Philosophy has always thrived on extreme, if not gross, examples. Says a colleague, often, to his introductory classes in ethics: "You think morality is all relative? Well, then, what if I think it is morally right to smash you in the head with this?" And he pulls out a hammer, waves it above his head. He is rarely without this hammer; it has become his trademark. (Nietzsche, when telling us how to philosophize with a hammer, had, I believe, something else in mind.)

Is this why W loved the flicks? The cool, hard, passage through extreme circumstances. Humanity tested at its edges.

A criminal investigation, however, must have a resolution. A philosophical investigation never will. Or at least never the right one. (Many innocent ideas will be brought mistakenly to justice.)

Philip Kerr, in his thriller *A Philosophical Investigation*, exploits these connections, building a mystery based on such fragmentary clues. He writes: "my thoughts were soon crippled if I tried to force them on in any single direction against their natural inclination.—And this was, of course, connected with the very nature of the investigation. For this compels us to travel over a wide field of thought criss-cross in every direction."[24]

So the detective becomes a philosopher fortunate enough to be blessed with a logical problem that is possible to solve.

Who is the killer, and how can he be found? There are a wide range of clues, and the field must be trampled delicately in all directions. Logic is an extrapolation from experienced reality, and fiction can be as well. Kerr's novel takes place in a not-so-distant future, a few years past the turn of the twenty-first century, where things are just a bit more extreme than even our extreme present. Crimes are more gruesome; murders are more violent, sicker and more gory. The macabre methods of serial killers are described in detail as Kerr delves into the history of this especially English obsession, all the way back to Jack the Ripper.

It is not entirely a surprise to imagine a future where weird killings are even more the norm, with a special homicide division set up for the investigation of such lurid cases. In Kerr's version, the best detectives are women. Why? Conviction more than 75% of the time. With women the majority of victims, a woman who knows the business seems to make a more diligent detective.

I do not find the extreme nature of the hunt-and-kill, find-the-culprit story inherently interesting. The obviousness of the resolution seems to detract from the ambiguities of philosophical mystery solving, where the plot is never the point, where the resolution is never final, and emptiness remains in the gut and in the mind. Chief Inspector Isadora Jakowicz feels she knows the difference between the philosopher and the detective: "For the detective, nothing is ever truly itself and nothing more." A discarded map, a still-burning cigarette, each shard of experience a clue to a happening, not a fragment of reality appearing mysterious in itself. The sleuth leaves the questions behind in the need for an answer. Rumination is never enough in itself.

The killer is called 'Wittgenstein.' He has been code-named 'Wittgenstein' in an experimental trial of a drug treatment plan for men determined to be genetically susceptible to violent crime. In the trial's secret database, some participants have been named for famous philosophers, and our villain seems to be killing them off. Coincidence?

The arrogance of the present is the wish to eradicate the ideas of the past, to bury our sins as metaphysical nonsense. Kant, Spinoza, Locke, Russell. All these code-named characters have been bumped off by 'Wittgenstein.' He is an intelligent murderer. Well read, if misguided. Tainted by logic, one might say. For our purposes what's important about him is how close the thoughtpaths of philosophy may swerve toward madness. Just after he shoots 'Descartes,' he reflects:

> "It's true, no one has interfered with my freedom. My life has drained it dry. A lot of fuss about nothing. This life has been given to me for nothing. And yet I would not change. I am as I was made. But I can still savor the failure of a life. After all, I have attained the age of reason. But what kind of reason have I to assume that my gun will fire if my finger pulls the trigger?... When I ask this, a hundred reasons present

themselves, each drowning the voice of the others.... And yet the same mind that is capable of reason produces monsters."[25]

The novel plays games with philosophy. Each recounted death of a code-named individual twists itself around that character's thought. A kind of revenge on the undergraduate years. Descartes doubts—everything except the primacy of reason. And in the indubitable existence of the thinker is contained the possibility for murder. A sickness only possible with detachment. *And this fragmentary way of thinking encourages detachment.*

The thoughtstyle of the 'real' Wittgenstein is seductive to so many. He offers a method that the mainstream has ignored in favor of what he is trying, unsuccessfully, to say. As he himself said, what he doesn't say may matter more. What he cannot say, oh how he struggles *not* to say it. How words are turned into walls that shape silent rooms out of the unspeakable. W's original unspeakable was the patterns we ought to live by, and how we tell what is beautiful and right. For Kerr the unspeakable is the darkness inside the human mind, the potential that allows us to kill for the sheer sake of it.

Are we all so intrigued with murder? We watch it for entertainment, we find it an overwhelming focus of popular and unpopular culture alike. I catch myself often being lured into the scene of a crime. I feel guilty, finding myself taking in so many unreal deaths all the time. Is it an excuse to avoid contemplating the real, less photogenic, unanswerable kind of death for which there is no one to blame? There! I will die, I know this, and whose fault is it going to be? Lock 'em up. Turn 'em every which way but loose.

I will not apologize for having been introduced to philosophy through *Monty Python's Flying Circus*. These are my earliest memories of history's great thinkers: the soccer match in which the ancient Greeks play the Germans. ("Look, there goes Socrates, he has an idea... he's kicked the ball.") Or the philosophy department of the University of Wallamaroo, Australia. Everybody named Bruce. "Rule number three. There is no rule three." Or, "Hello, I'd like an argument, please." The Pythons want their revenge on philosophy as well.

Even back in America, I seem to remember in the margins of *Mad* magazine strange references to someone called "Nietzsche." Why was this funny? Why is philosophy funny? Because it represents ultimate seriousness, something beyond amusement? *Don't be embarrassed, this is where we began. Neither bang nor whimper but laugh, above the lazy hum of a B&W tele-tube, and with cheap magazines on the back-of-store racks.*

Was Wittgenstein ever funny? Remember, he thought one could write an entire philosophy composed of jokes. Some readers think his whole enterprise is a joke. Others find it as serious as murder.

If philosophers are all mind and no body, then they have always gone about murdering each other. As Kerr has his killer 'Wittgenstein' say in a pontificating "Lecture on

Murder," given over a satellite virtual reality network, it's a wonder any of them are still thought of as living thinkers:

> "Today it is even more obvious just how much good can result from the murder of one dusty, arid, old philosopher. Both Marx and Freud were murdered by Jaspers. Bertrand Russell and G.E. Moore should have been murdered by Wittgenstein, as Ramsey certainly was. Heidegger died very properly at the hands of A.J. Ayer... And Chomsky, well Chomsky may turn out to have killed nearly everyone he came into contact with."[26]

We can speak of ideas killing one another and it sounds exciting. Vanquish and conquer, the urge to demolish. Yet this arrogance, too, is a sickness. Philosophy teaches critical thinking, and then it runs from the response. So there's a problem: how do we build a solution out of the remains of the dead idea? One idea after another, one hunch after another left a goner by the side of the road. What, then, can we believe in? What destination can we look forward to? Philosophy itself is dead when it offers nothing but trouble.

I have thought about systematically removing the word 'philosophy' from this entire narrative. It seems to scare people away. Not because it sounds dangerous, but because it suggests again an unfortunate distance. Its conclusions and illuminations should be close to all of us, yet we are frightened at how lonely they've become. At the end of the thousand pages there is no prescription but the message to think for yourself. There are instructions to get you started, but no end product, no magic spell.

If you meet W on the road, kill him. Like Buddha and the rest. Do they only exist to die? And remember, W passed through his torture and lived on! His last words will still reverberate: "Tell them I had a happy life." He enjoyed every moment of the struggle. (At least, when looking back upon it.)

Inspector Jake takes a trip to Cambridge to ask an old don if the culprit might have studied philosophy in his youth, and if this could have contributed to his sinister madness. Professor Lang replies, "Chief Inspector, you've no idea the kind of strange people who apply to read philosophy. To paraphrase Keats, they are the kind of people who would clip an Angel's wings."[27] Why? Because they do not want to believe what they see? Or to demolish all myth and drag its bodies back to Earth?

All around me I see philosophy becoming destructive, while feigning innocence in its own way. Shooting down belief in cold blood, standing for nothing instead of something. Encouraging inaction instead of action, because change cannot always be explained or justified. Often those who take it most seriously cannot connect it to the progress of their lives. They become stuck in graduate school, because to write the diss. and get out is somehow a compromise of their own quest to get beyond belief and into the very structures of thought. I find them mistaken, but my motives may be impure. The life-and-death struggle in pure abstraction may not do much for mundane existence. It may make it impossible to get up at all—at least without savaging someone else's intent.

Kerr has it in for philosophers here. Perhaps they did something bad to him once, so he wants to watch them all die, in his own metaphorical way. He knows his stuff, and has transformed it into something creepy and new. Read it yourself—I don't want to tear it apart so much as see what its mood suggests to my own worries. Novalis once called philosophy "a kind of homesickness." A need to feel at home everywhere. But without the tools, the wherewithal to fix things. Just to point to the holes in the ceiling and the rot in the foundation. Is that enough? I hope instead to offer new ways to see things, different routes to make sense of the boom and buzz of it all.

You'll see, there's a message here—somewhere, in between the lines—of hope.

How will they catch the killer 'Wittgenstein'? I give away no secrets. Only failed strategies. Perhaps they might persuade him to kill himself, instead of innocent victims? Isn't that what all this dissatisfaction is about, an inability to live with oneself, to accept the logical conclusions of one's sins? The philosophy don and the inspector consider testing this option. The man has done so much damage to the world that Prof. Lang hopes he might end his own torment. Jake wants a proper trial; still, she's got the Cantabridigan on line with "Wittgenstein" over some virtual reality contraption, baiting him, stalling him, as the police close in:

> "I'd be correct in assuming that you believe in God?" [says the professor to the serial killer].
> "Yes, you would be correct...."

"I won't ask you why. I'm not interested why. But I'm sure you have your reasons. Whatever they are, I respect them. I feel quite sure you must have given the matter a great deal of thought. But look here, if you really want to wave two fingers in the face of God, then you've been missing the point. [Murder]'s not the way to do it. To flee from existence itself is the most critical sin, the ultimate rebellion against the Creator. What is required of you is intensified defiance, the heightening of despair. The last time we spoke you described yourself as an artist. I don't doubt it. Only as such, yours is a common dilemma: the sin of living life in the imaginative as opposed to the real world, of Art instead of Being."

Wittgenstein sighed. "Perhaps you're right," he said wearily. "What you say about the artist's existence feels true."[28]

Wittgenstein-killer is a believer. Wittgenstein-philosopher could never quite bring himself to believe. (Later, Thomas Bernhard will also compare two distinct Wittgensteins, one the consummate thinker, the other the consummate madman.) And even after three of his brothers killed themselves, he could never accept the solution of suicide. Perhaps this is what keeps philosophers alive so long: they endure in the hopeful world of the question, and cannot rest because however many answers emerge, there will always be more questions. In a letter to his friend and architectural collaborator Paul Engelmann, the real W writes on June 21, 1920:

I know that to kill oneself is always a dirty thing to do. Surely one *cannot* will one's own destruction, and anybody who has visualized what is in practice involved in the act of suicide knows that suicide is always a *rushing of one's own defenses*. But nothing is worse than to be forced to take oneself by surprise. Of course it all boils down to the fact that I have no faith![29]

We are here catching the real Wittgenstein in one of his worst periods. After the Great War, running from philosophy, preparing to take his teacher certification to head for the most rural possible parish to seek solace among 'real' people, untainted by the malignant pressures of a seething Austria. His restless wandering in search of a career and place that he can live with may be just what keeps him alive. He will one day return to philosophy and the stunted academic culture that surrounds it back in Cambridge, but he will never quite fit in, and will continue to urge his students away from a life of the mind.

And W, murderer? He has not got long to live on the lam. I'll spare you the details. You see, he too has picked up the tone of W the philosopher, but without the moral gravity. Brother Wittgenstein the sole survivor is the man who would not compromise his beliefs (oh yes, he did have them) and kept searching for the place that would have him, a place he also could accept. His obsessions were pure, his sins were the facts of being human. He told us not how to live but how to stop life in its tracks. And find the questions that freeze our existence in doubt. To leave space for the deepest feelings to well up, unspeakable.

Stay mum on the most important things—a resigned but thoughtful silence. This makes the limits of one's language the beginning of one's world. Is this the alter-Wittgenstein, slayer of life or of logic? Kerr's man offers these final words from the beyond:

> "What can I tell you about what it was like, lying in that drawer one lifetime, and then gone somewhere else, I don't know where? How can I describe it to you? The picture is something like this. Though the ether is filled with vibrations the world is dark. But one day man opens his seeing eye, and there is light."[30]

A novelist friend of mine has told me that certain writers' styles are infectious to him. He reads their work and finds he wants to write just like them. James Salter in particular grabs him this way; he has to shake himself to get free of *A Sport and a Pastime*. Wittgenstein's way has the same effect on me. I seem less interested in what he said than in how he said it. Like a disease, the style infects me and then at times becomes an annoyance. It is too cold-blooded, too calculating, too easy to slide towards murder, of one's confidence or one's dreams. The questions are thrown up in the air so poignantly as to *resist* answer. To paraphrase Marquez, "There can be no way out of this labyrinth!"

You do not want education to lead to madness, or to any dissolution in the faith absolutely necessary to accomplish anything of worth. And do not rip off the wings that are still able to take you away from here, anywhere, anywhere, as long as it is out of the world.

"One can't drink wine while it ferments, but that it's fermenting shows that it isn't dishwater. You see, I still make beautiful similes."[31] Midway through his life, Wittgenstein congratulates himself. These comparisons of his are either Zen-like stabs at the truth or witty games with language. They could be poetic if he would let them, but W insists that he cannot write a line of verse, that the poetic is a *goal* for philosophy, somewhere over the horizon of how he conceives his own work.

A goal for me as well: some idea of how to continue philosophy so it does not melt so easily into air. It's the future, and it's only beginning. Still, it is easier to destroy than to bring something to life.

xpresses [illegible] (logical) form.

; 4.121. Altho we can give merely a formal def. of form of prop^{n} as that
ch is common to 2 facts one of which can serve to represent the oth
is impossible to tell in significant prop^{ns} what the logical form is
m is ultimately inexpressible & is a part of the mystic.
timately form should be grasped by direct intuitional insight.
ell. hesitation in adopting this inexpressibility of form. But Russell misses the p
as in mind not any one symbolic syst. w.i. the setting of another & larger
the fund. expression of all possible symbolism, and in such discourse we
ly cannot put ourselves outside all symbolism. Hence hierarchy of langs. solu
twork. Also R's uneasiness about fact that Witt. managed to convey s.th. ab
le due to confusion between 'to say' and 'to show'; Tr. merely makes us cs. of fund.
l. From the very nature of logic as the consistent use of symbols, a
logic itself cannot be significantly symbolized in its turn.
her, a consistent use of symbols is logic or expresses the logic
a logical statement P shows itself to be logical. A statement
to say this about P does not do it any more than state
itself. At the end of any explanation we have to come to
thing which we cannot explain any further; and logic,
ested in any rational discourse whatsoever, cannot be exp
its turn by a discourse but has to be grasped intuitive
it is present

gical form of reality: the grammar of our language through which
the world (no 'ultimate' properties of reality involved if
speaks of the logical features of the world he simply means
logical' or grammatical properties of the lang. which reflect
are applicable in the world)

is one of the mystical aspects of reality. While it is by virtue of
prop^{ns} represent reality, the form itself cannot in turn be repre
not by other propositions
must be grasped intuitively

take a fact p, and a proposition p_1 representing it; p and p_1 ha
m in common. In understanding p_1 we grasp this form.
assume that we fail to understand p_1 and that p_2 is used
plain it. Then in understanding p_2 we grasp the form comm
p_1 and p_2. If we do not understand p_2 we continue until
get to p_n which we do understand. The form of p, p_1, p_2 ha
vanished from p_n but propagates itself thro all the series & reappe
p_n. But at the end of the series we still have to grasp this form
by intuition. Hierarchy of langs. suggested by Russell & Carnap
not eliminate the necessity of direct grasping of form

IV:

Obvious Secrecy, Visible Screen

In 1993, *Wittgenstein,* a film depicting W's life and ideas, was released by the British director Derek Jarman, a victim of AIDS known for his application of "queer sensibility" to portrayals of England in our century. Wittgenstein was homosexual in a secretive, protected and tormented way; Jarman's vision is self-consciously and visibly queer. Some have said W would roll over in his grave if he saw it. On the other hand, if he were alive today he might have a life far happier than the happy one he avowedly had. Or he might be confused: finding himself encouraged to be overt about a part of his being that was essential in its secrecy. One of those things of which one must remain silent.

A poet is one who is remembered more for her lines than for her ideas. Or for how the fleeting complexities of thought are captured in phrases that seize on accident. W as poet and as uncompromising seeker become the hero of accounts like Jarman's. How he could never rest, how he dragged along all those around him at least some of the way—this power cannot be ignored, and might be exemplary in some sense. Many of those who come across the story try to make sense of it, write their own versions, insert the growing legend into our own lives.

In the book version of the film, we are presented with two scripts, the first by Terry Eagleton and the second and final one by Derek Jarman and Ken Butler, responding to Eagleton's first foray. Eagleton's is based on the most narrative moments of W's life story and ideas, while the final version goes for the hidden sensibility, those things previously silenced, presenting the mood of the man by way of his thought, what it can picture and what it only erases.

The most dramatic moment in Eagleton's version is when Russell storms into W's rooms at Cambridge to call him to task for encouraging a working class kid to give up philosophy and find a menial, 'real' job in a factory and thereby give up philosophy. W in real life berated philosophers constantly and encouraged all his students to leave the field if they possibly could. (Otherwise they would find no rest.) And what of those students whose parents struggled so that they could escape a life of drudgery and pursue instead an intellectual course? How dare he try to send them back! "Do you hate yourself so much?" bellows Russell in the script. "Do you realize the power you have over people!?" Not wanting disciples in the least, W finds they flock to him. He gives no solace. Tells them to go back where they've come from. There is no salvation, or even solution, in philosophy.

Is it natural for philosophers to detest their own field? Such self-loathing seems more common here than in other endeavors. This may be because philosophy reminds us that we, as a species, as a multiplicity of thinking cultures, haven't got much of a clue as to what's going on. We can live our lives all right, but at the core we do not know why we have chosen certain premises instead of others. Philosophers point out these problems and then are shouted out of the room for it. We skulk around, looking elsewhere, searching for a place to fit in. Homesickness, homesickness. You will not be able to feel at home everywhere. And does choosing just one home always entail compromise? Things must be assumed, other things must be left out. There is no resolution or completeness. But there may be *resonance* with the surrounding indeterminacy. That can be the feeling of wonder itself.

There is no doubt that W has *inspired* many. He has been an important model, voice, and above all puzzle. His relentlessness is a mixture of integrity and madness, though he kept forging ahead and never decided to end it all, like three of his brothers. He and Paul the pianist survived.

Eagleton as Marxist would tend to find the intellectual's backing of the worker's life particularly fascinating. Is he then criticizing himself by emphasizing this irony in another's struggle? W was no Marxist himself, nor member of any group that would have or spurn him. He wanted to be alone—his sympathies for simplicity came from Tolstoy, intuition, and a lifelong quest to escape doubt.

In an earlier novel, *Saints and Scholars*, Eagleton dreams up the unlikely meeting of W and James Connolly, martyred hero of the Irish republican rebellion, in a stone hut on the Irish coast. No doubt the point is to muse on who is the philosopher, who the people's champion. And how the revolution might be viewed from the extremity of language cold as ice. In reality Connolly was shot in Dublin, but in this story he gets one brief last respite with Wittgenstein, and the theory of revolution is pitted against its practice. Here's W thinking to himself near the end of it, after Connolly has been apprehended a second and final time:

> The more simple, the more complex: a barren life breeds fanaticism. *What if philosophy and the people are not strangers?* Connolly is a common man, yet a philosopher. A crank, maybe; but a crank is an instrument which makes revolutions. What if he is right that the crisis is common? The people will de-

ride this folly, live on in the innocent self-evidence of their gestures. There is no resurrecting the dead. If the dead rise I am done for. I thought I had touched rough ground, but there may be bog beneath.[32]

That is my question too, the drawing together of the populace and perplexity. Not yours for the revolution, I will be yours for the question. Which, like the revolution, will never be over. W had a deeply felt sympathy for the cause of communism, though I believe it was intuition, not conclusion. This would have been one aspect of the man to film; the sparseness, though, is another.

With Eagleton's script as raw material, Jarman took the risks that only someone concerned with art more than documentation could take. W himself is raw material for those bent on making sense out of him.

Throw out those questions up into the sky. Some will take to the wind, and others will return with the tide.

Jarman's film is shot entirely in a studio. Black backdrops, a feast of colors set against characters and emptiness. It is mannered, sketchy, just playful enough to save itself from wry dogma. It would have made a wonderful, almost magical play. As cinema it seems stunted, but so is its subject. It is a philosophical commentary, more lucid than many. Already with his introductory notes, Jarman has been infected by the aphoristic style:

The floors and walls of the small studio draped like a funeral. A black infinity. The minimum of props and settings. Blues, reds, violets. There is one moment of set dressing. Break your own rule.

The film was pared away. I was always removing things. It is the same with the soundtrack. A process of elimination.

Mark of the Naïf? No distinction between Bertie, a table, and a rhinoceros. All alive and equal.[33]

Eagleton ends with W wishing he could write a philosophical work consisting entirely of jokes. He can't because he admits to no sense of humor. J begins with as much humor as he can wring from this bleak character, while still being true to his genius.

W's many references to bright, garish colors: red, green, blue. For Jarman these are clues to bright decoration against the black room of the film studio, in front of the blackboard of inquisition.

What matters is what we can't say, implies W in his most quoted sentence. We can, though, show the truth, reveal it through oblique blinds. Wittgenstein sought salvation in film, mostly cheap detective thrillers whose plot offered some kind of relief from the agitation of the seminar. "Film felt like a shower bath, washing away the lecture."[34] Jarman's film is a different sort of solution, with a more circuitous plot: one where the fly leaves the fly bottle but somehow gets back in.

J begins by showing things W never spoke of. Childhood. We see a young Wittgenstein, dressed up in Roman costume finery. Laughing, horsing around the room like a precocious nerd. We are to see how a child's imagination might have lead to the race from one impossibility to another—a thinker striving time and again to escape his fate! There's even a Martian in this film: Mr. Green. Naked, painted green from head to toe. This is the kind of character W might have thought up were he ever a child. Was he a child? Did he ever speak of a Martian? He did, toward the end of his life, in *On Certainty* and in the *Remarks on Colour*. As a foil to the human race, a being to whom *everything* about us humans would need to be explained. How we know. What we see. How we decide. The very strange components of our world.

Red, green, blue. A film of primary colors, the mixtures of light radiating through the camera lens. The best thing about this film is that it does not try to depict the life of Ludwig Wittgenstein in any straightforward manner, but instead uses his life and style as inspiration for a series of staged vignettes. The inner world of W is made manifest through the acerbic story. The picture does not hold us captive, but attempts to show how the ideas are linked with the life. Jarman is another person who has learned from W by picking up fragments, making his own whole rather than imagining one is there to begin with. There is no picture, not even a frame, not even a declaration of many frames waiting to make images out of experience, but an aesthetic echo to the arresting peculiarities of a life so severe it cannot be ignored.

Severe only in subtlety, hard-edged only at the core, the blades facing in. Outward a piercing gaze. After any articulation, silence.

The three women in tight lycra bike outfits: red, green, and blue. Giving W the finger. Or fingers. One or two. "Fuck you" or "victory." He does not know what either symbol means. A combination of confusion and contempt for women? Not so much contempt as indifference.

Elizabeth Anscombe was just about the only philosophical woman W could tolerate, sometimes even calling her "old man." She tried to get him interested in Kafka when they first met. W gave back the books: "This man," he said, "gives himself a great deal of trouble not writing about his trouble."[35] And did Wittgenstein ever write about his trouble? Privately, yes. Outwardly, no—this may have been the most important thing about which he needed to remain silent.

In his trap of a picture, Jarman chooses to keep the women at bay. The eroticism of men, however, is given the forefront. There are, for my taste, a few too many scenes of dark-eyed, swarthy Johnny wearing leathers and polishing his motorcycle, but it is definitely a point of view, one that could be culled out of the secrets of Wittgenstein's unwritten troubles. (This Johnny is no recognized lover out of W's own life, but a kind of fantasy composite.) We do have of course the famous coded remarks, personal comments interspersed in the whole of W's piecemeal writings. Ray Monk, in his copious biography, has been smart enough to intersperse these notes among all other references, so if we want to find them we'll have to sift through the whole volume and will not be able to isolate his sexuality from the rest of his amazing life.

His relationships reflected a kind of cautious obsession, and a need to be authentic whatever might happen. There was nothing garish about W's sexuality, but there might at times be a kind of philosophical closeness. He did not want any of his lovers to be philosophers. No, they must all in the end contribute something useful to society. And in this process they would leave him.

Wittgenstein alone in his spectacular retreat, poised on a steep slope overlooking the Sognefjord in Norway. The proper scene for extreme thoughts and realizations. It is 1937. He writes from the cloud of loneliness: "I would now like to live with somebody. To see a human face in the morning.—On the other hand, I have now become so *soft* that it would perhaps be good for me to have to live alone."[36] Again, weighing forever the pull of opposites. His friend Francis Skinner visits him at last, and for once in his life W writes of the physicality of love: "Lay with him two or three times. Always at first with the feeling that there was nothing wrong in it, *then* with shame."[37] He seems afraid that going out on a limb for love, out to the edge of the precipice, will make it disappear and in its place will come an emptiness. If only philosophical conundrums could disappear so easily! Then his work would be done. And it never was.

If there is any difference between Wittgenstein's sense of sexuality and anyone else's, it might just be that his sense of relationship existed most firmly in his own mind. As simile. Once again standing for something else, a rigor or an ideal, far past the precariousness of actually being human.

The men in W's life drifted away from his harshness, and many died young and tragically. That happened more in those days. Now we tend to survive so long, still around to wonder.

"I think constantly of you and of the wonderful time I have had with you. It was wonderful that it was possible. It was so lovely being with you and living in the house with you. It was a wonderful gift to us. I hope it will do me a lot of good."[38] A letter to Francis, afterward. Straining in language to make it so simple—but the bond between questioners never is.

Nine years later it is not clear whether W has learned any more about how to accept love. Writing of the young Ben Richards, he feels the closeness he needs with others will always pass: "But I am easily hurt and afraid of being hurt, and to protect oneself in *this* way is the death of all love."[39] Only in philosophy does all the injury come from within. "A person cannot come out of his skin. I cannot give up a demand that is anchored deep inside me, in my whole life. For *love* is bound up with nature; and if I become unnatural, the love would have to end."[40]

The ideal is a hidden ideal. W is anchored in secrecy, defined by reserve. In thoughts he analogizes, forces out insight. He wants to explain the hopelessness of his love by claiming that it is unnatural. In fact it is not so much against nature as unsettling—like any kind of love. Bringing an other so close to his life might upset the grand quest to explain. Questions might find a way of getting answers, and a feeling of settledness might quell the noble ascent toward doubt.

Games, games, why can't the man come to terms with the truth!

In W's need to write away his sins and thus absolve himself of them, I am strangely reminded of Benjamin Franklin's similar attempt, where we see this avowedly practical early American intelligence indulging in the same kind of relentless self-scrutiny that took hold of Wittgenstein. For there was a time in this stove-building skirt-chasing kite flyer's life when he decided he was at last going to set himself straight:

> It was about this time I conceived the bold and arduous project of arriving at *moral perfection*. I wished to live without committing any fault at any time, and to conquer all that either natural inclination, custom, or company might lead me into. As I know, or thought I knew, what was right and wrong, I did not see why I might not *always* do one and avoid the other. But I soon found I had undertaken a task of more difficulty than I had imagined.[41]

From here Franklin goes on to attempt a method of accounting with respect to thirteen important virtues, keeping track in a small red-inked notebook of his performance over time during the summer of 1733. Each week he focused on one virtue as the prime subject of his holding-back, while trying to do his best with all the others. He kept this method going sporadically for years. Note that in his comments under virtue number twelve, "Chastity," the remarks are only ". . . ." Somehow numbers two, "Silence" and thirteen, "Humility," over the long run have more weight. I imagine Wittgenstein would have been at first intrigued, then tormented, by such a method.

I quote these longer excerpts from the "coded remarks" because they are of topics W tended to shield himself from in the public eye. There is a need to search for the warmth behind the icy surface of the personality. But love is here for him an inner problem that he wants to attack through relentless consideration of points of view of the self. He does not ask of others, or otherwise try to learn, what they are concerned with. These lovers or would-be lovers suggest inadequacies within, and show how philosophy becomes psychology when fired back upon the inexplicitness of deepest and lingering desire.

Jarman wants to put all this out in the open. W only puts out the questions he wants the students to learn to spurn. And all they do is follow him!—to the ends of the earth? In his camp-filled colorful staging of Cambridge intellectual life of the period, J does put on a show that I do not think W would find amusing. But it is as much a picture of a time and place as a drama of a man whose plot lines were hidden more than overt. W's notion of a relationship—be it a human or a logical one—is something internal before it is a happening with a result. His world went on inside him.

The documentation of it that we may now assess is only and always will be imperfect. Thus so many make stories around him out of these fragments.

The more I delve through this material the more it seems that everything I am writing, whether inside or outside this manuscript, deals with these same fragmentary footholds on understanding. *Perhaps it is that way for you, too? These pieces are now indelible for our culture. We can't push them away into a box, we cannot forget them once we have heard.*

He traveled incessantly, dreamed of escape, seeking a peace perhaps impossible for a thinker at large on this earth. In Moscow he wants to become at last a manual laborer. Professor Sophia Janovskaya offers him a possibility of two professorships, which he will have nothing of. J has her tell him, "We must teach the frozen circumstances to sing by playing them their own melody."[42] A little creative imagining of what W might sound like were he Russian, with a metaphor that sounds translated from a foreign tongue. After Wittgenstein, the stunted sentence begins to sound more normal. I picture the society held in place by a solid coating of ice. When the right wind blows, the entire edifice sways as a whole. The branches and pinnacles begin to move, and the shackles crack and melt away. Only if you can guess the tune.

Jarman has John Maynard Keynes intone the parable of Wittgenstein's life and its two-part course, told as a story that the philosopher-as-child can take in:

There was once a young man who dreamed of reducing the world to pure logic. Because he was a very clever young man, he actually managed to do it. And when he'd finished his work, he stood back and admired it. It was beautiful. A world purged of imperfection and indeterminacy. Countless acres of gleaming ice stretching to the horizon. So the clever young man looked around the world he had created, and decided to explore it. He took one step forward and fell flat on his back. You see, he had forgotten about friction. The ice was smooth and level and stainless, but you couldn't walk there. So the clever young man sat down and wept bitter tears.

But as he grew into a wise old man, he came to understand that roughness and ambiguity aren't imperfections. They're what make the world turn. He wanted to run and dance. And the words and things scattered upon this ground were all battered and tarnished and ambiguous, and the wise old man told him that was the way things were. But something in him was still homesick for the ice, where everything was radiant and absolute and relentless. Though he had come to like the idea of the rough ground, he couldn't bring himself to live there. So now he was marooned between earth and ice, at home in neither. And this was the cause of all his grief.[43]

The young Wittgenstein, all exactness and solution. The older, restless wanderer, no way to live in the grit of reality once he's felt the polish of truth. Isn't this the opposite of what they all tell us, and isn't it so often just like this? The young are actually naïve enough to believe that there is a system, a way, a game whose rules describe precisely how to win every time. And then once experience has taken hold of us, begun to fill the infinity of possible memories, then we know that is just one way the world looks to us at one time, from one angle. Shift your gaze and all icebergs groan and crack in the springtime sea! It happens each year without fail. Each time it becomes more familiar, and more beautiful. Too bad—we have become philosophers before our time.

And then you might say W's mistake was to try to *live* in the world he had depicted. It might serve as an image, as a picture to be held captive itself, not to hold us in its spell. It was not life philosophy he espoused, but instead ways to look at things once we step back from them. He never wanted to offer clear advice to himself or to anyone.

Jarman's film should not be watched as an introduction to the philosophy or life of Ludwig Wittgenstein. It is more a wry commentary on everything about him that can be packed into images on a screen. When I said it would have made a better play than a film, that's because everything that happens is so conveniently staged, and if coordinated right in front of a live audience it would have seemed so immediate, even magical. On film I somehow wish for more. There is certainly a vast range of visual possibility in the man's life; he could almost be the subject of an epic film, instead of an insular one. Two world wars, global fraternal suicides, spectacular locales, continuous and restless escape, always cutting to the chase. The ideas could appear as a voice over to a whirlwind adventure—Ludwig of Europa! The danger of philosophy, cast down through mist, echoing down the fjord, smuggled out of the prison camp, carried home by gulls from the far Irish coast. The cool commentary could serve as a foil to the true tumultuous life.

That, maybe, would be the kind of film W would have liked to see, worn out and muddled after a lecture he never wanted to give in the first place. For the philosopher, it must be remembered, did love the flicks.

V:

Shameless
Characters

Thomas Bernhard has the distinction of being the only person, so far, to write *two* novels about Wittgenstein. And in a sense, all his works are a response to W, as well as to Austria and to his own intractable self. Bernhard is W's stylistic opposite, as most of his fiction is composed of single paragraphs that extend for hundreds of pages. Like W, though, he does not make like easy for the reader. None of his books are about ease in the least. They are concerned with difficulty, once again the difficulty of surviving through the struggle of our time. And his are the roughest answers we have found so far.

Everyone in Bernhard novels is either slowly dying or fighting to finish studies, dissertations, or artworks that have no beginning, middle, or end. Someone is usually ill with lung disease, as Bernhard himself was much of the time (it finally killed him at age fifty-eight in 1989). His work is full of relentless self-examination of the internal Austrian consciousness, and his celebrated will reflects his antipathy to his adopted land:

> Whatever I have written, whether published by me during more lifetime or as part of my literary papers still existing after my death, shall not be performed, printed or even recited for the duration of legal copyright within the borders of Austria, however this state identifies itself.[44]

So upon his death as a much debated playwright and literary figure, he closed off his work from his own country for fifty years! Did he hate his country that much?

He once signed a guestbook as "goodness in person," and he firmly believed that his deeply depressing narratives should have a cathartic, uplifting effect. He died by assisted suicide, but only after decades of battling the sickness that so consumed his characters and himself.

His works graft his own ailments onto the lives of public figures. In *The Loser* he has reclusive pianist Glenn Gould die of a lung illness he never had in real life. Bernhard has a way of imposing himself onto the very possibility of external characters and happenings. He does not want to get away from the inside, and in his novels there is nary a conversation, just stream-of-consciousness inner monologues that roll on for page after page.

It is easy to get depressed by that stuff if you devour the novels one after another, as I have done. But the secret is to look once again for hope, for strategy, for understanding. This man had guts, to write himself into existence this way. He had a sense of humor W might have appreciated. (As Wittgenstein said of Freud, "It takes one Viennese to know another.") But W, as a fan of fast-paced detective stories, would have been appalled by the copiousness of it all. (He would have been agitated, too, and would have found easy reasons to ignore it.) Page after page, ream after ream. Muddle, muddle. If he couldn't take Kafka, he surely would not have accepted Bernhard, who does not slice through his own problems but swims into them, laughing as he is surrounded with the encasing of dread.

Is this the kind of great literature that is good for us, and has to be rammed down the throat? I can't imagine

Bernhard ever being popular in upbeat, happy-go-lucky America. From inner Europa he is an achievement, a perfectly shameless chronicler of his own war inside. He does not practice self-analysis, because he does not want to be cured. His sicknesses, physical and mental, are the "experience" that fuels his art. He is angry at what Austria has become, and the national sickness is what he wants to cure.

I would hazard the guess that it is the determination of Wittgenstein that impresses him the most. And the battle to escape his Viennese-ness that took W all across Europe, and to Moscow and America. The theme of running away, in order to accomplish what must be done. (And the utmost courage necessary to stomach any return.)

Bernhard's best-known novel, *Wittgenstein's Nephew,* may not be fiction at all, but a memoir of his friend, Paul Wittgenstein, who, in B's account, does for madness what uncle Ludwig did for philosophy. The uncle unburdened himself of his financial fortune, and the nephew tried to cast away his intellectual fortune. But the intellect, unlike money, remained inexhaustible. Fortune smiles? In this passage Bernhard writes around the historical Wittgenstein myth and places himself candidly inside the narrative as well. As always, we cannot tell if it is true, but it seems searingly honest:

> ...Paul's mind quite simply exploded because he could not discard his intellectual fortune fast enough. In the same way Nietzsche's mind exploded, just as all the other mad philosophical minds exploded, because they could no longer sustain the pace. Their

intellectual fortune builds up at a faster and fiercer rate than they can discard it, then one day the mind explodes and they are dead. In the same way Paul's mind exploded one day and he was dead. We were alike and yet completely different. Paul, for instance, had a concern for the poor and was *also* touched by them: I too had a concern for the poor, but I was not touched by them; my mind works in such a way that I have never been able to be touched as Paul was...[45]

This paragraph is ninety-seven pages long, and constitutes the entire book. And yet the story leaves me like an aphorism, a sad reflection of two friends who never quite got to say to each other what they really meant to each other.

It is the opposite of W's rushed shorthand pronouncements on friendship. It is the recounting of the incredible effort it takes for two so self-willed people to make contact with each other, to figure themselves out in the presence of the other. Bernhard writes that when he met Paul Wittgenstein his first thought was that he had "a name which I had revered for decades like no other."[46] The second thought, or the thought that came over time, was that he was a person unlike any he had ever met. Where W finds companionship an impediment to pure thinking, Bernhard finds philosophy through the discovery of friendship. They are thus after different kinds of philosophy, with different notions of how primal ideas need be separated from the screaming needs of the self.

The infectious nature of Bernhard's style is a deeper, slower kind of illness to come over one. He asks not for the glimpse, but the digging into the dirt of what happens as the foundation of what we know. If he is to be a mentor or model, then we should all write our own lives into the subjects we study, the people and things we are interested in. We should feel comfortable going on and on, recounting again and again the same things that have happened to us, imagining that they happen in the same way to all the people we would like to pay attention to, who we would want to acknowledge us as part of their worlds. It's not that no detail need be left out, as in the fastidiously complete narratives of a Proust, but that the pain should be opened, peeled back just at the point where it hurts the most. The most empty view of the human condition can be projected onto the way the world appears, and the story will go on and on and on, and any attempt to break it up will close down the swirl. I cannot yet do it, I don't catch the fever. I look straight ahead, and still see spaces between the words and the emphatic outbursts called paragraphs. On the indented handholds of their ends and beginnings, I use that space to hold on. I need to rest, to see how high I have climbed, before deciding whether to press on or to jump.

Bernhard denies me this pleasure, or this chance. With his words, it's all or nothing. They stream out of him, and I have the sense that he has a hard time stopping them. Is the river edited or marked up? Themes repeat, phrases come back, as in the music he practiced in his youth. But it is a tone poem in words, not a theme with variations like this present story. One senses that the books have a beginning and end only because that is the convention: otherwise they could gestate as nothing but middle, an unassailable consciousness just *there*, ruminating constantly.

Long before he met Paul Wittgenstein, Thomas Bernhard considered Ludwig Wittgenstein as a kind of hero, whose story was worth recasting. W took some part of the genius of Vienna and offered it to the world, without compromise. His family offered him every consolation, and he had to spurn them to avoid killing himself like all those brothers. W could stretch his thinking out on a limb and decide that the analytic work mattered more than self-discovery. Paul, perhaps adapting some of the terminology of his uncle, saw too much of his own situation, and was driven mad by *"the whole dreadful picture....* The one was *possibly* more philosophical, the other *possibly* more mad.... I would go so far as to say that whereas the one *published* his brain, the other *put his brain into practice....* In either case, the Wittgenstein name guaranteed a certain standard, indeed the highest standard."[47] The message is that if one thinks too much in the actual world, the best will be unable to survive. If you transfer your torment to literature, frozen (if swirling) words upon a page, you will be remembered. And will you have a happy life?

The debate recurs forty pages later, still in the midst of the same paragraph: "One might say that [Paul] made an early getaway, as his uncle Ludwig had done years before, abandoning everything that had, after all, made them both possible, and transforming himself, like his uncle Ludwig before him, into what the family regarded as a *shameless character.* Ludwig transformed himself into a shameless philosopher, Paul into a shameless madman."[48] What drove uncle and nephew to equally relentless pursuits? The same thing that drove Bernhard on without shame, that great Austrian dream of self-obliteration that pulls the individual up out of the water at the moment before drowning. "In our country," writes Bernhard in *Correction*, "suicide is commonplace."[49] Almost to be expected from the tormented. What takes courage is to stay alive. Bernhard fought death all his life, and perhaps believed that the battle scars gave him a certain right to find a specialized way to write out his demons. The sickness might be made bearable by projecting it onto the lives of the sufferers who surround him, or else there would be no need to pretend that his ailments would interest others in the least. He is writing himself into the book of survivors, feeling betrayed by those who, like Paul, die because they are too extreme. Lacking a tablet on which to inscribe their genius, they scarify themselves. They do not know how to separate life from art. Neither does Bernhard, but at the bottom of it all, you should see he is laughing. It *is* obsessive. As such we should enjoy it, a window onto a sufferer *shameless* enough to publish it all for us to puzzle over.

The book is a desperate report of the deep and simple closeness possible between two friends. Bernhard and Paul were linked by a black suffering throughout their short lives. They often found themselves together in different wings of the same hospital, one there for disease of the lung, the other for disease of the mind. They might softly pad the corridors to find the other, to express condolence.

Suddenly, though not expectedly, Wittgenstein's nephew is gone. So much for the living link to the shameless possibility of these black sheep of the esteemed Viennese family. Bernhard is left to hypothesize his life alone, and he summarizes his philosophy of the turning-away:

> ...There are times, however, when life is endurable, and at such times we occasionally manage to count three or four people to whom in the long run we owe something, and not just something but a great deal—people who have meant everything and have been everything to us at certain critical moments or certain critical periods in our lives. Yet we know that as we get older we have to employ ever subtler means in order to produce such endurable conditions, resorting to every possible and impossible trick the mind can devise, though it may be stretched to the limits of its tolerance even without having to perform such unnatural feats. Yet at the same time we should not forget that the few people in question are all dead, that they died long ago, for bitter experience naturally inhibits us from including the living in our calculation—those who are still with us, perhaps even at our side—unless we want to risk being totally, embarrassingly, and ludicrously wrong, and hence making fools of ourselves, above all in our own eyes.... Now that I have no living person left, I tell myself, I will face the January cold and the January emptiness with the help of the dead, and of all these dead there is none closer to me, at this time and at this moment, than my friend Paul...[50]

There is safety in eulogizing the dead, for few will dare to criticize your memories. Especially when the memories end up on paper, published and classified as 'fiction.' The result is read for a well-told tale, for the beauty of the language, but never for accuracy. So much easier to wax lyrical about the dead! They will not arise to disclaim how we have portrayed them, and whatever evidence comes up will do nothing to contradict these moments itemized in language.

These thinkers and artists are not trying to prove anything about the true and only Wittgenstein. They want to make use of his obsession, to explore the *possibilities* inherent in a life made up of a series of extreme questions. I want to show that the vast array of responses to such never-ending queries constitutes the way philosophy is assimilated as a relevant, accessible if troubling part of culture.

For Bernhard the story is a relentless puzzle, hard to keep straight from book to book. He is compelled to write it again and again, like a thinker banging her head incessantly against the same wall. His novel *Correction* can be said to take off from this curious fact from Wittgenstein's life: although never trained as an architect, he designed a house for his sister Gretl in Vienna, a material monument to the embodiment of logic, less so life. Bernhard's character Roithamer builds a house deep in the forest for his sister in the form of a perfect Cone, so perfect that nothing before had ever been created with such perfection. Roithamer is an architect, scientist, polymath, professor and researcher at Cambridge, that same place Wittgenstein reluctantly called home. Roithamer is in fact obsessed by W, so clearly an alter ego for W that the character is emphatically a vehicle for Bernhard to deal with the eccentricities of the real in the person of a created fiction.

The difference: What else? Roithamer killed himself, hanged from the rafter of the perfect Cone where no one ever lived, a secret, mad project never understood and already abandoned to decay. This novel is another relentless paragraph, a reeling cavalcade of madness scraped together out of shards of historical allusions. The clarity of the English university, the fatal neuroses of the Austrian forest. The dichotomy of bringing things to life and forcing oneself to die. Roithamer, a philosophically-minded architect of the type there may be far too many of these days, thought that "the word B U I L D is one of the most beautiful in the language."[51] And it's written just like that, with the characters spaced out, so that the letters become like edifices, solid columns and buttresses that will not fall under the crush of impossible syntax and the stream of consciousness that threatens to deny the syllables the space they need to breathe. Roithamer seems able to expound endlessly on the elucidation of words, though the central core of his scientific work is never explained. The man goes mad. He writes pages and pages explaining why it was essential to the world for him to build a perfect Cone in the middle of the Kobernausser forest, at "the exact center of the forest at an angle he had calculated for months."[52] The impression we get is of a man consumed with a fanatic passion for something pure and exact, hence impossible to live in, having no place in the human realm of architecture. And the story rants on...

"Enclosed you will find a few photos of my house and [I] hope you won't be too much disgusted by its simplicity." So W wrote to John Maynard Keynes after the completion of his architectural foray.[53] It is a sparse, Bauhaus-like structure, devoid of ornament yet manufactured to the tolerance of millimeters, with special-order window sizes and lined metal rails and gratings. It represents a purification of the noble lines of Vienna's stately mansions, the style of domicile favored by the wealthy Wittgensteins. The course of abstraction that led to its modernist lines can be seen in these sketches of W's design partner Paul Engelmann, who shows how the clean lines of logic come right from the flutings of a more decorative style of life and of thought:

The inside of Wittgenstein's house abstracts even further to become a volumetric composition of nothing but forms:

Inside it contains a most remarkable *radiator* that fits in a particularly tiny corner:

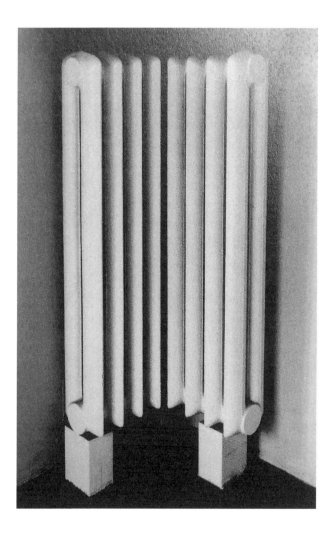

Apparently it was quite expensive and difficult to construct:

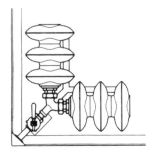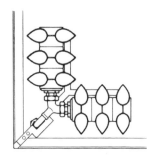

We wouldn't want a philosopher to be backed into a corner, now would we? This is far from the chilling madness of Roithamer's Cone, but fiction at times needs to push reality to further extremes. The real philosopher's sister did live in and enjoy the house—until the Nazis forced her to leave. Today the building is used by the cultural affairs branch of the Bulgarian embassy.

Just another cold, stark modernist building? Here, ornament has been transmuted to detail. There are no mistakes. There is no room for "allegories of the time," as Gretl herself called the paintings she *thought* of hanging up. But the design must be unobstructed enough to be a monument to itself, to the problems the designer himself was working through at the time: "Philosophical work—just as, often, work in architecture—is really more working on oneself, on one's own outlook, on one's way of seeing things. (And what one expects of them.)"[54]

And one expects that art should not remain as therapy. It transcends its first function and is left for others to use. Even in present photographs the place is unable to explain itself.

Why is each peculiar facet of W's life worth a whole imaginary exploration unto itself? The shorthand suggests possibility—we may nod with disapproval that here was a genius who *did not make use of his full potential.* That is a modern therapeutic view. This guy was a mess—"He could have been helped." Yet the life also contains much for sheer admiration, beyond the logical achievement. This man would not compromise. And if his *was* a happy life, then he took a perverse delight in proving to the world that his standards were too stringent to fit in. His life was devoid of furniture, his work a struggle in the realm of questions that continue on without end, in a room with a table and a chair and nothing else—no books, no distractions, no outside thoughts to intrude. The inner puzzle is enough to occupy forever those who see it.

Bernhard's Roithamer is a swirling Wittgenstein to the *n*th degree. His life is, predictably, described as a maelstrom of obsessions, a crazy mind roiled by all subjects at once, because "unless one is thinking of *everything at each moment* one is not thinking at all, according to Roithamer."[55] Though this may sound like too much it is all that keeps Roithamer alive, and he chooses to focus his intractable energy on constructing this building that leads up to a point, the huge and perfect Cone, whose apex would concentrate his wide-ranging mind unto a single desire, a dream that he hoped would hold him together and stop his inevitable blowing apart. For how could such a man hope to survive in the sinking state of Austria, which Bernhard loved and loathed so, unable to support originality, unable to admit its own dark failings and withering national spirit? "...[T]his state has countless men like Roithamer on its conscience..."[56] Bernhard counted himself among them, writing and writing his revenge even after his life is over.

And this Cone, this demonically funny structure, leaping right from philosophy into architecture: It's the dunce cap writ large, the solo belief, the round crown in the forest, far from any other habitation, that goads us into accepting that we are all in the end so alone. No wonder sis couldn't even dream of life in it. If you believe this is true, you'll see the great mind writing itself into isolation, writhing at the need to include everything at each moment all at once. This strangely excessive requirement for the strength of a thought, combined with a gentle belief that each thought, however light, can be a great thing:

> We're up to something, as we know, it's invariably something stupendous, even our most insignificant, unimpressive brainchild is always the most stupendous thing, and we feel we must speak of it, go into it, and we're disappointed, either we're not understood, no matter how clearly and forcefully we put our case, or else we don't want to be understood.... First twenty-one chambers in the Cone, then eighteen, then seventeen chambers. A single chamber under the Cone's tip, with a view in every direction, but in every direction the same vista into the forest, nothing else. Three-storied, because a three-storied

edifice accords with my sister's character, 'my sister's character' underlined. Of the seventeen chambers, nine are without a view, among them the meditation chamber on the second floor, beneath the chamber in the tip. The meditation chamber is so constructed as to make it possible to meditate there for several days in a row, and it's intended for no other use but meditation, it's totally devoid of any objects, there's not to be a single object in the meditation chamber, nor any light either. A red dot in the center of the meditation chamber indicates the actual center of the meditation chamber, which is also the true center of the Cone. The radius from this center in every direction is fourteen meters long. Spring water on tap in the meditation chamber. Underneath the meditation chamber, areas for diversions. Above the meditation chamber, the circular chamber inside the tip of the Cone, affording views in all directions, but in every direction nothing but forest is to be seen...[57]

Relentless overdetermination, repetition and incessance. The sister is not allowed to see the house before it is finished, because of course she will run in terror. It is based only on an idea of her, not on what she might want. It is an empty, logical system writ large in order to clean out life. No room is to have furniture, no room (aside from the meditation chamber) is to be planned for any specific purpose. All is free, flexible, undetermined. Overdetermined only in the exact possibility of freedom, all at once, everywhere, all the time. The Cone is a similar height as the trees in the forest so it will be like some metal and technological tree, like those cell towers camouflaged as Frankenpines.

Invisible for miles around, impossible to glimpse until you are there. To find it: look for the exact center of the forest.

A crazed affront to nature that will be left to decay into nature after R's and his sister's deaths. So Roithamer has written in his will—once again the need to exert power over the living once we have left them. With this precise disregard for mortality comes a very strange attitude toward nature. Nature in opposition to the city is what saved Bernhard—he loathed the cultural dearth of the country but needed it to breathe, as his lungs could not take the pollution that is Vienna. He was forced to flee the festering capital again and again in his life. Yet the neurotic metropolis was his laboratory, and he wrote its obsession into the calm of the woods.

Tubercular Bernhard resented nature for making him suffer, and lived in the country only to survive. "In fact," he has written, "I love everything except nature, which I find sinister."[58] His retreat from nature is into the realm of the word, and he catches himself sinking into the lethal smoke-filled chambers of dark Viennese cafés, where he reads obsessively all newspapers, all fine print, all sideline stories of the empire's decay. Old news, but ever fresh when considered from within. Roithamer, only a slight fictional twist from his author, cannot take the rough insurgency that is nature, and goes for long stretches, years on end, absorbing nature only through reading matter, and thus comes to the forest with the dream of his insane and perfect tree of steel, which he will place in its center and insist that his sister dwell within. It's an imposition of logic against the rough earth, again the theme we have already heard, a dream of a planned world poised against the irregularities of life, the shudder and shock of the discovery that it can't possibly fit, with the tower shattered, the rusting hulk empty, and no one left who remotely knows what it was all about. "Build" may be a beautiful word, an admirable career, but now all R sees is "the *vulgarity* of building."[59] The nakedness of structure. Its sheer inappropriateness.

Surprisingly, there is a similar passage in the memoir of Italian writer Italo Calvino. As a child, taken out into the countryside by his father:

> And me? I imagined my mind was elsewhere. What was nature? Grass, plants, green places, animals. I lived in the midst of it and wanted to be elsewhere. When it came to nature, I was cold, reserved, sometimes hostile. I didn't realize that I too was seeking a relationship, more fortunate perhaps than my father's, a relationship that literature would give me, restoring meaning to everything, so that all at once everything would become true and tangible and possessable and perfect, everything in a world that was already lost.[60]

Calvino's remorse would later take him back to the natural world, where he would specialize in its meticulous description without rhapsodizing over its superiority. Literature does imbue the implacable with readable meaning. For Calvino it leads us to smile at what he is able to convey of what he sees, while for Bernhard we can laugh only at how deeply he has gotten himself into what can't be seen, but can't be forgotten. This human nature is no place to visit, but the home of doubt inside us.

I smile, sucked in to the brilliance of the obsession. I too am in the forest, and suddenly realize that the house I write these passages in, this one that I have borrowed for the summer of 1996, is in the shape of a pyramid, two pyramids actually, right angle pyramids, joined together at the hypotenuses. It is no outlandish structure, probably built out of plans from *Popular Mechanics*, many windows, all looking out at the woods. No sound but the gentle munch of carpenter ants eating away at the walls. Bernhard would have a field day. Yet he is also too depressing for this beautiful place. Wittgenstein wrote of logic in places like this: Rosro, Sognefjord, Wicklow, Storey's End, away from it all, in silence, with space in between the words for the unspeakable to grow. Choose to put madness onto paper or to live it instead.

Twenty years later this fine wooden house in Maine is long gone.

Maurice Drury's recollections of W depict a man very different than the W of public imagination. These, the most detailed reminiscences written by any of Wittgenstein's friends, show a highly cultured man with opinions about much of the science and literature of his time, even the history of philosophy! Drury describes respect for Spinoza, Leibniz, even Dickens. It seems not to be true that W cared only for detective novels and American films.

"You think philosophy is difficult enough but I can tell you that it is nothing to the difficulty of being a good architect. When I was building the house for my sister in Vienna I was so completely exhausted at the end of the day that all I could do was go to a 'flick' every night."[61]

Back in Bernhard's fiction, Roithamer's sister sees the Cone at last, she is horrified, and the sight of the construction of his view of her inner structure precipitates her slow decline into death. A mistake, an aberration, a mad inclusive idea. Roithamer writes on toward his own end. Believing first and foremost that "a body needs at least three points of support, not in a straight line, to fix its position"[62]—this fragment of geometry grafted onto the non-Euclideanism of human existence—his own fragile balance tips. He has been thinking about too much too much of the time. And yet if aware of all this how could one make do with less? We have to see what we see. If you see too much you must couch the vision in an utmost belief in life, in survival, in the continuation of oneself so that a difference may be made. Then you can tell everyone else what you see.

Not that they will pause to understand, not that it would do them any good. The need to go on should be paramount if one wants to seek the truth but does not claim to have found it. When the quest does damage, though, when it destroys people because you have been captivated by an image instead of what is wished for by others, then it may well be too late. As it becomes for Roithamer, whose own conical persona crashes down as he has no more light to look up to:

When a body is acted upon by external forces besides its weight it tips over on one side of the base... We always went too far, so Roithamer, so we were always pushing toward the extreme limit. But we never thrust ourselves beyond it. Once I have thrust myself beyond it, it's all over, so Roithamer, 'all' underlined. We're always set toward that predetermined moment, 'predetermined moment' underlined. When that moment has come, we don't know that it has come, but it is the right moment. We can exist at the highest degree of intensity as long as we live, so Roithamer (June 7). The end is no process. Clearing.[63]

The nobility of the severed life is that it offers this closure that lets go into the open, the clearing in the forest, the empty circle where the Cone could have been. Instead there is a free space where one of our many human trees formerly stood. At this point we have to make the choice whether *to inhabit process or leave it behind.* Bernhard always insists that suicide is a mistake, yet he seems to profess admiration for the lack of shame that drives someone to a personal end upon the grounds of incessant and misguided brilliance. These glass bead games of interleaved concepts make better stories than moral codes. No one could live by the order of the Cone and so it will rust away. We have forgotten the "shameless madman" who thought thousands would attend his funeral. Only a small circle of people were there. Bernhard was not among them.

His, though, is truly a literature of the unwritten spaces between the aphorisms of his idol Wittgenstein. These seething torments are the flip side of the questioning filters that point out the possibilities for a beyond-human world, seen in flickering colors, the green visible in growth and the red exposed for decay. B does not believe in silence in the presence of those wrenching troubles of life that lead words to falter. The *struggle* to write these roughest edges onto paper was his lifelong adventure, and this documentation lives on. It is the most poignant corollary to W's cold observations that I know.

And in its darkest moments, this tidal wave of prose can still make laughter out of death's inevitable victory.

Leif Haglund
Wittgenstein Drawings

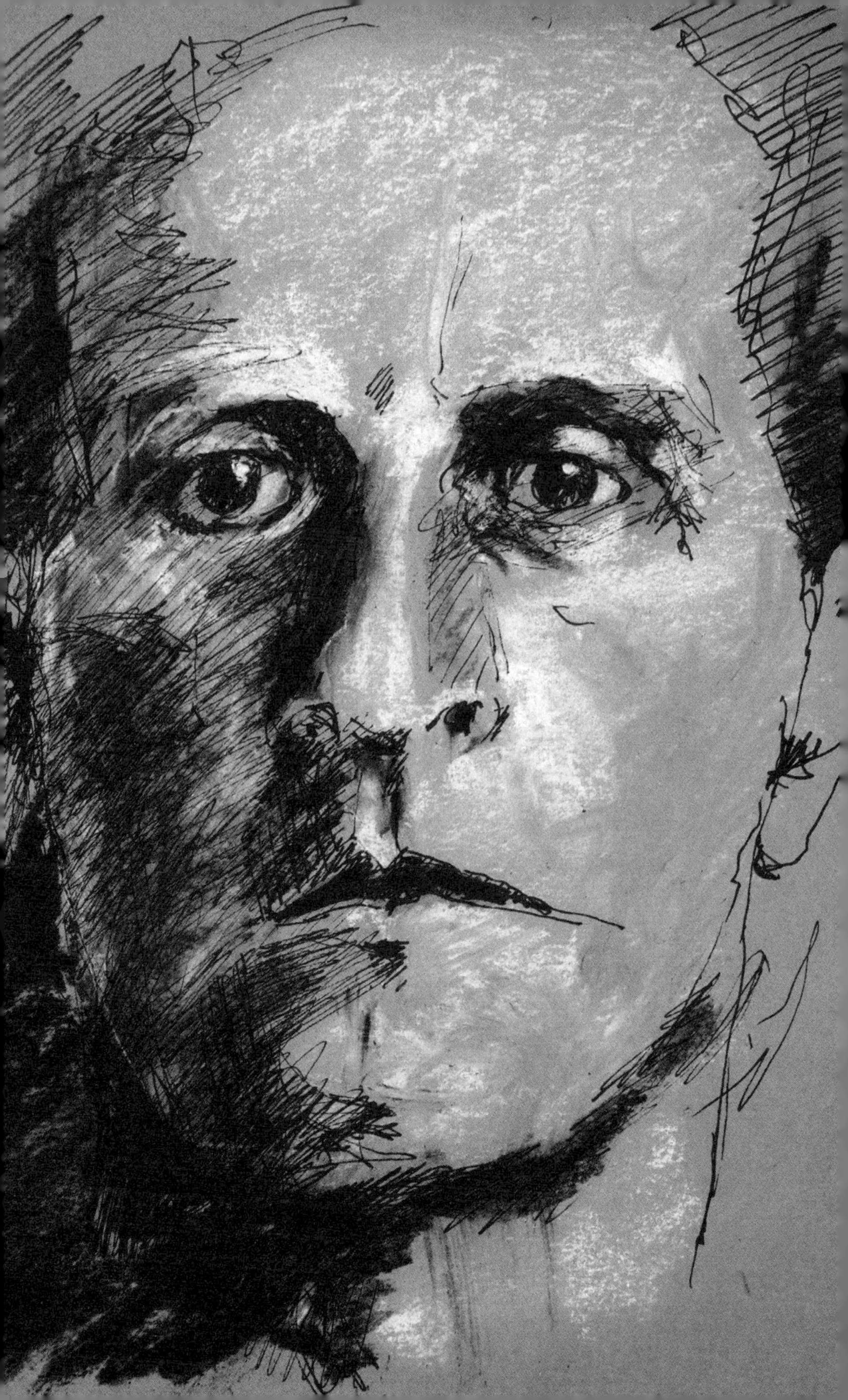

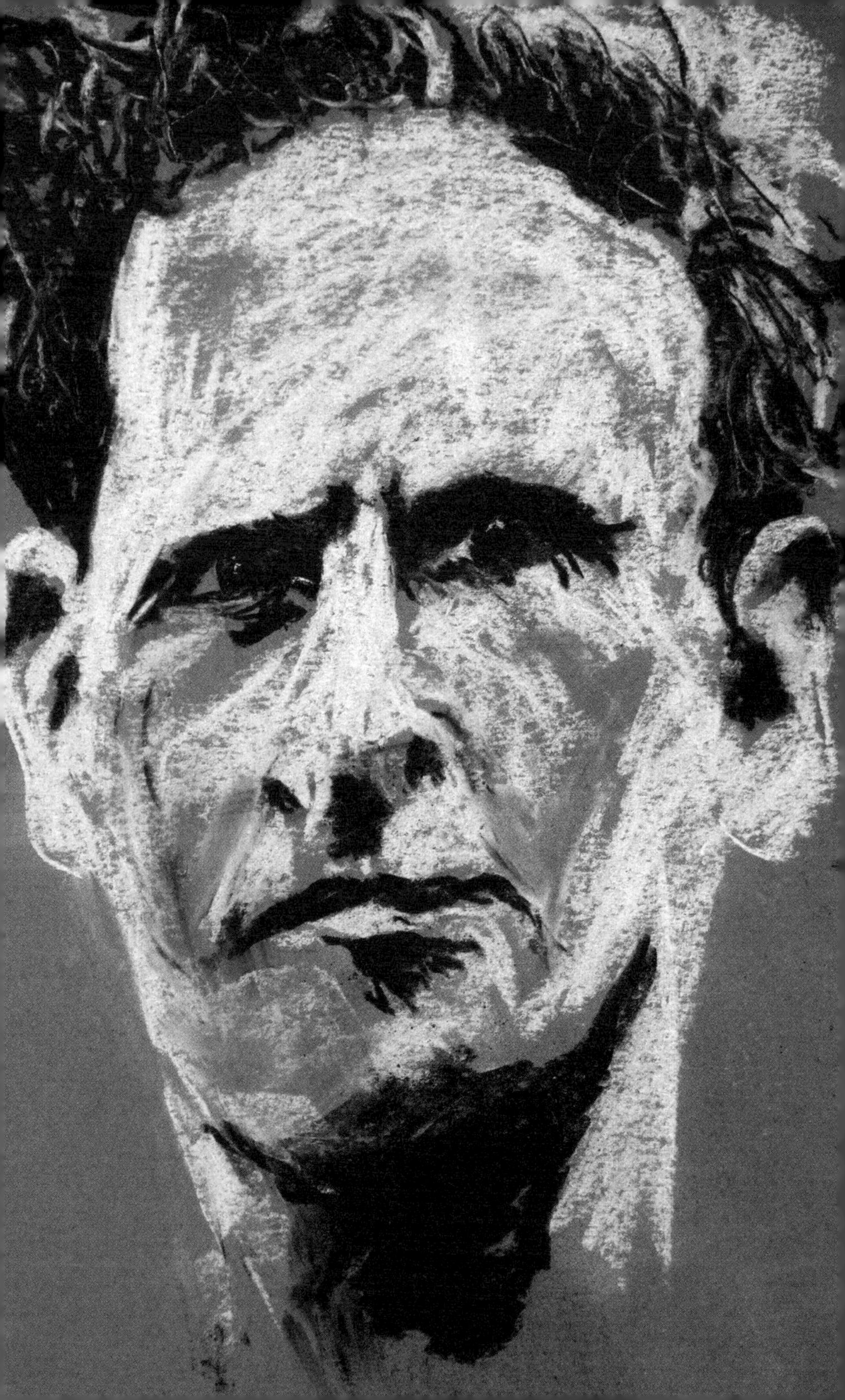

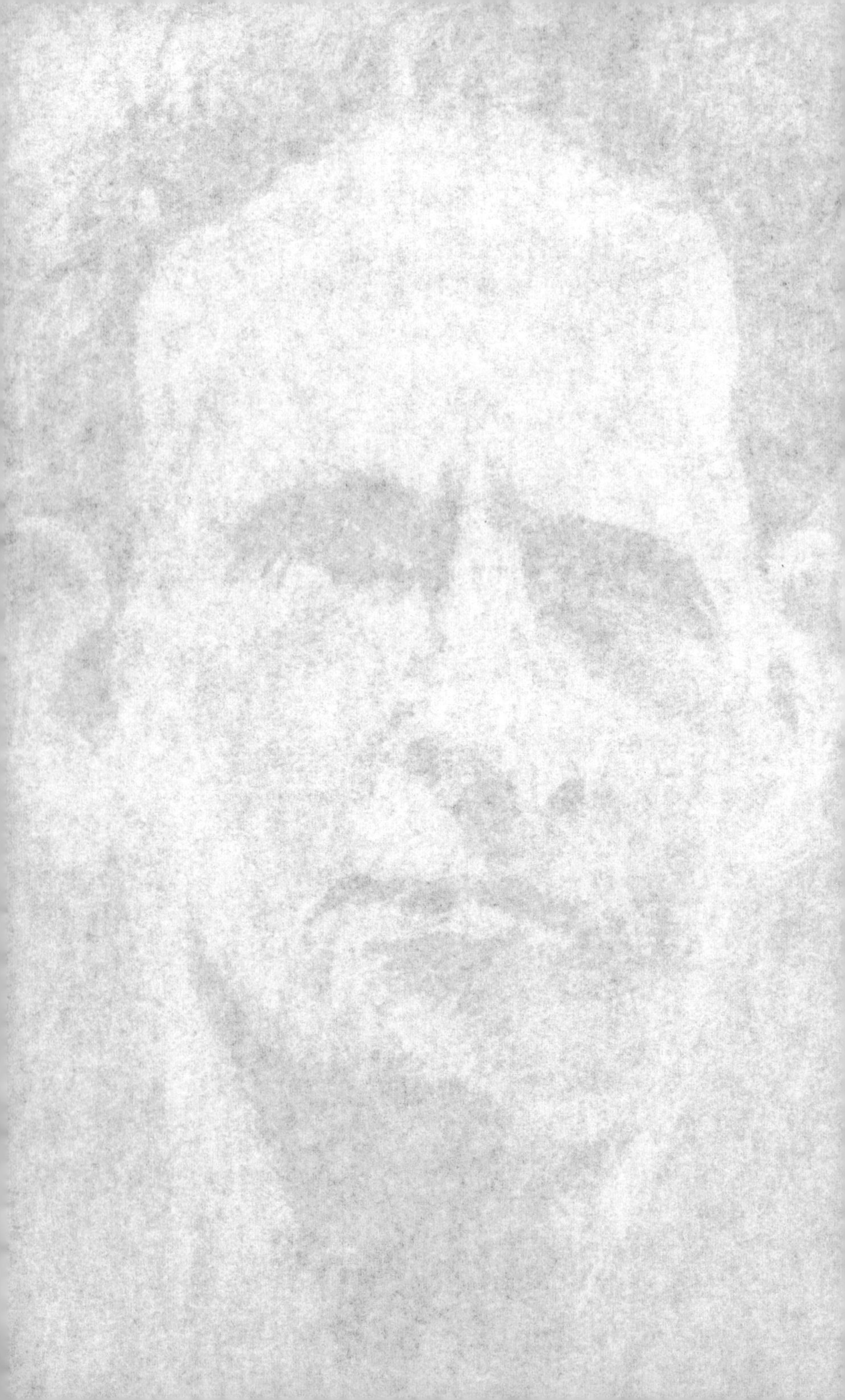

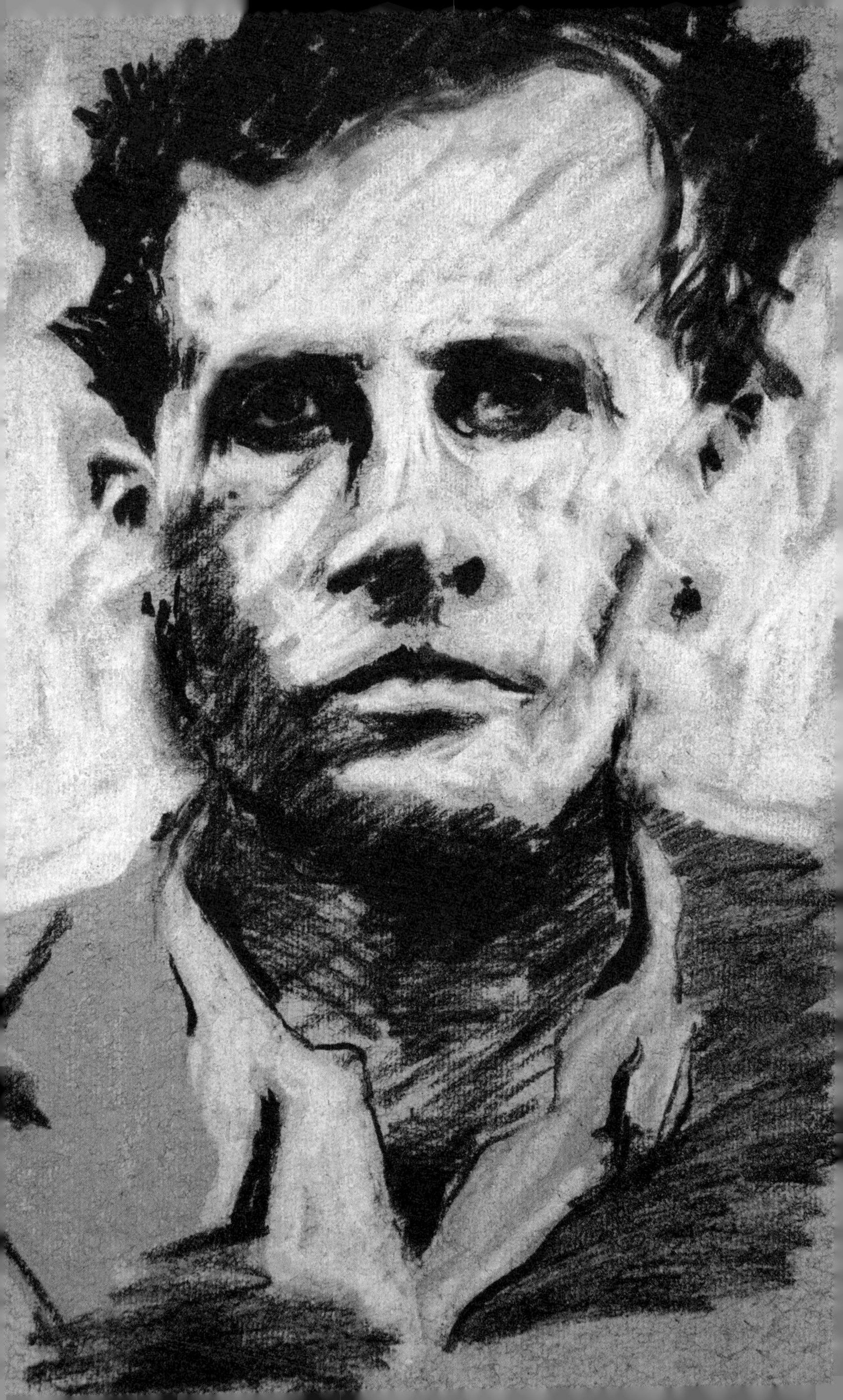

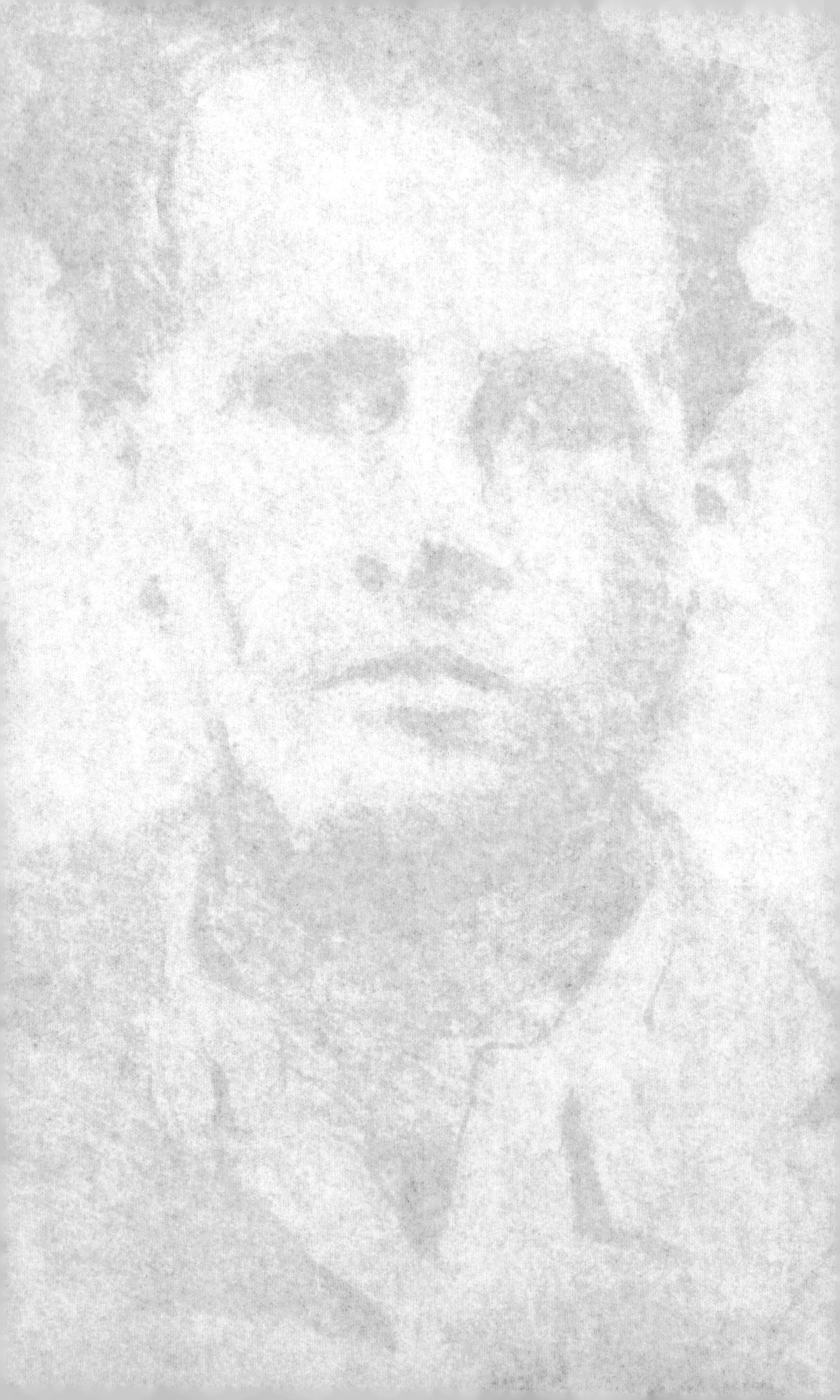

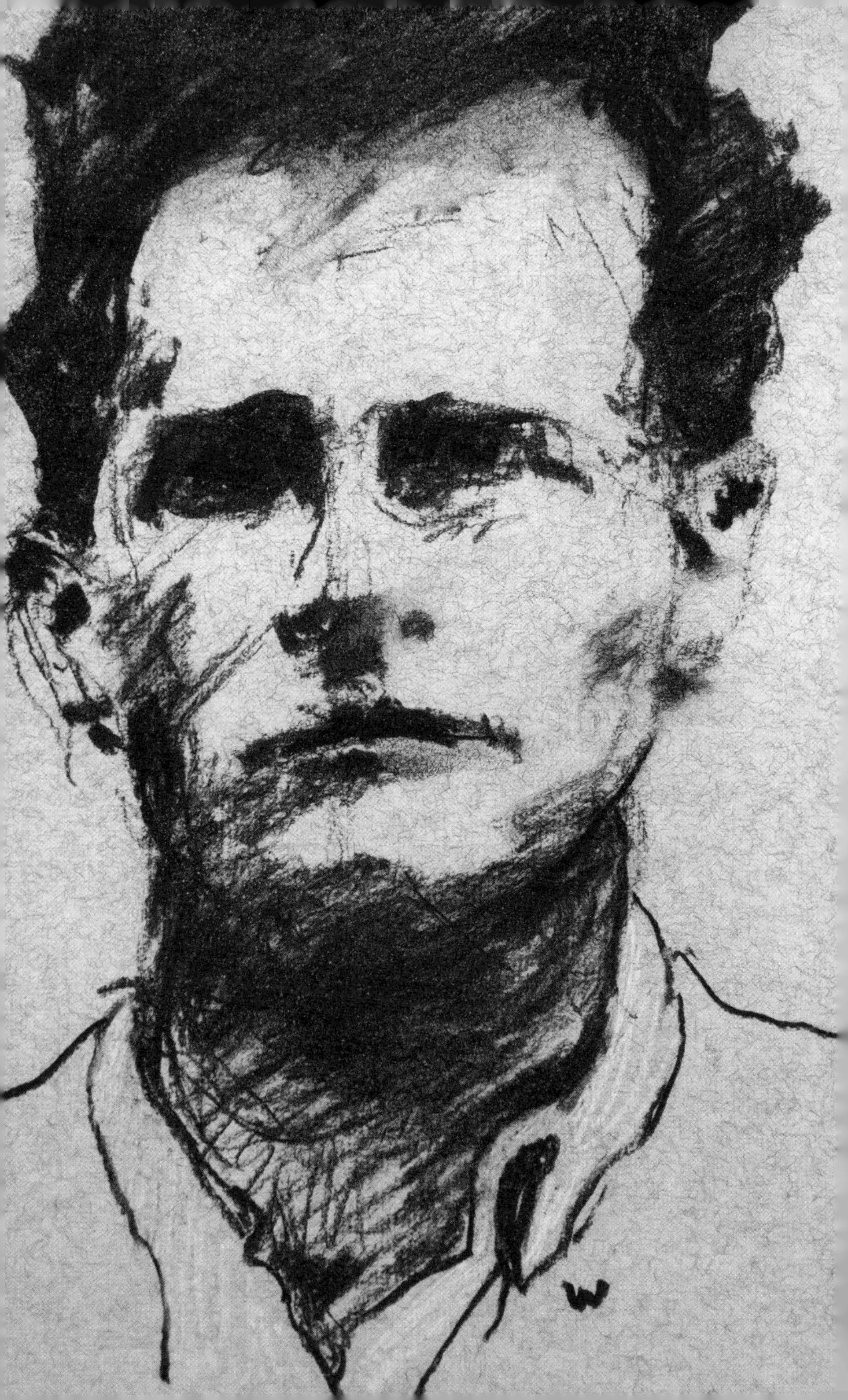

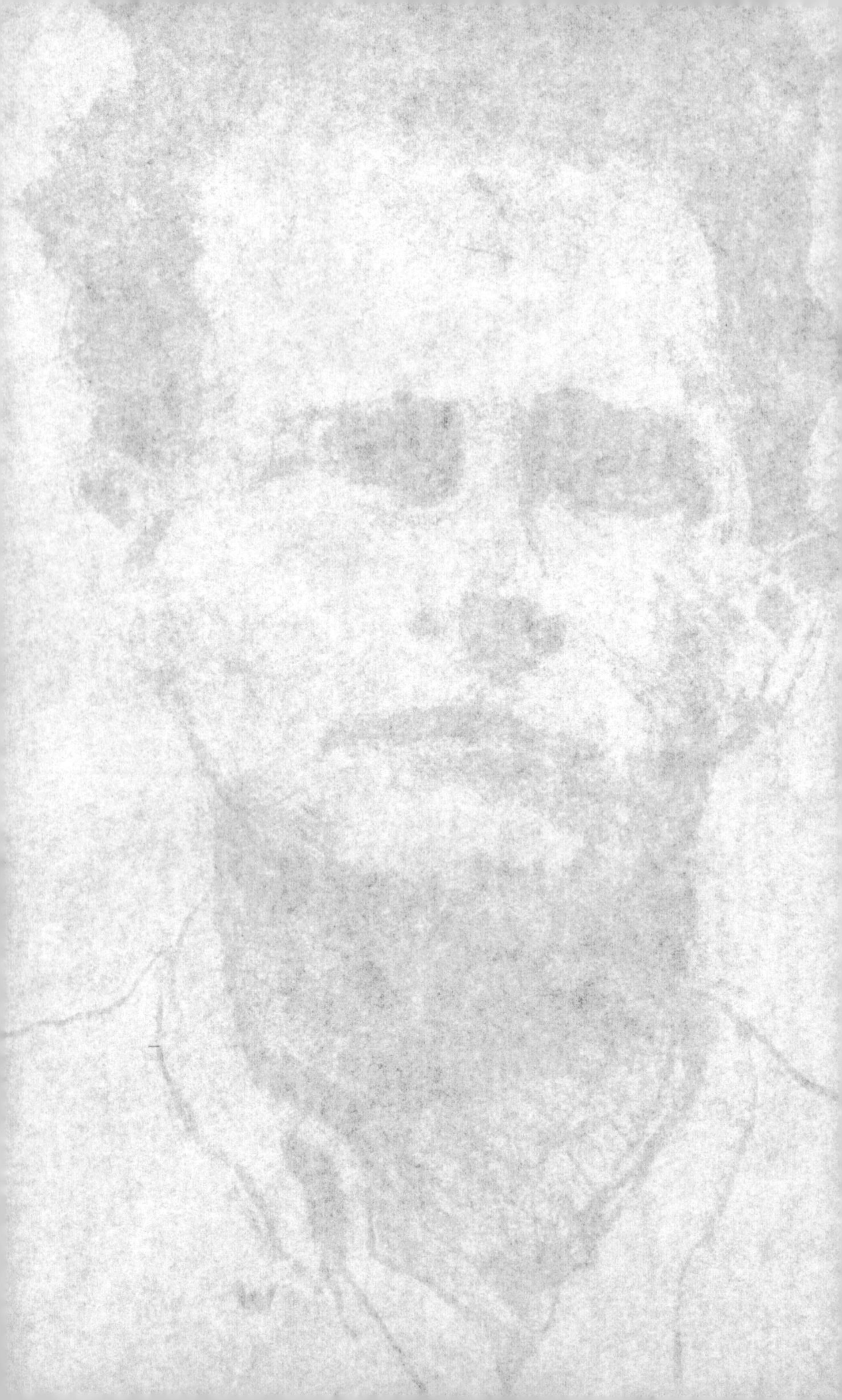

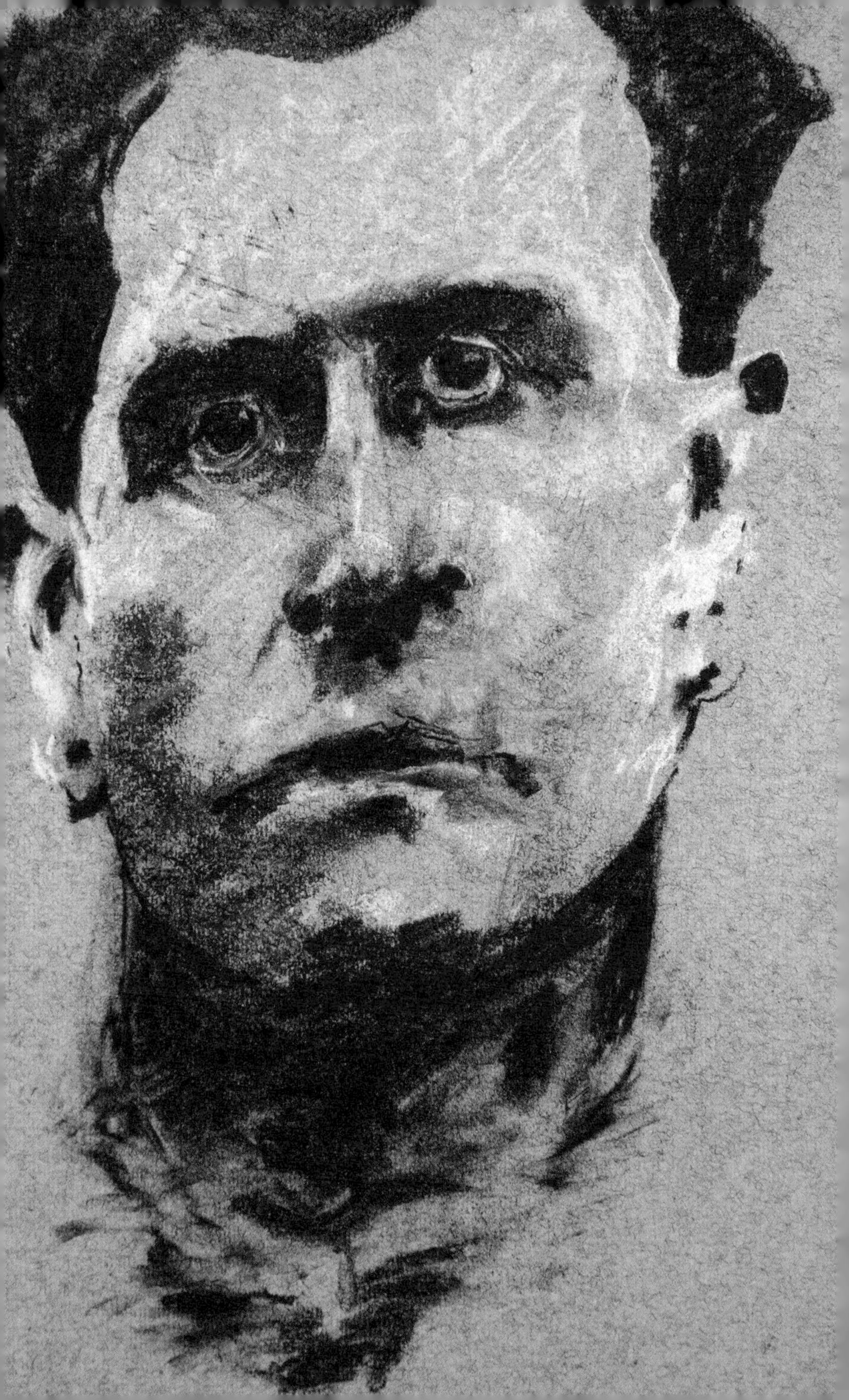

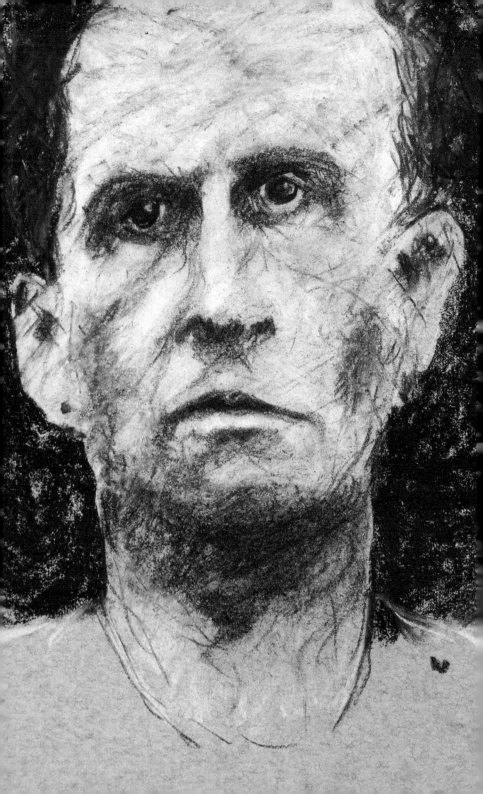

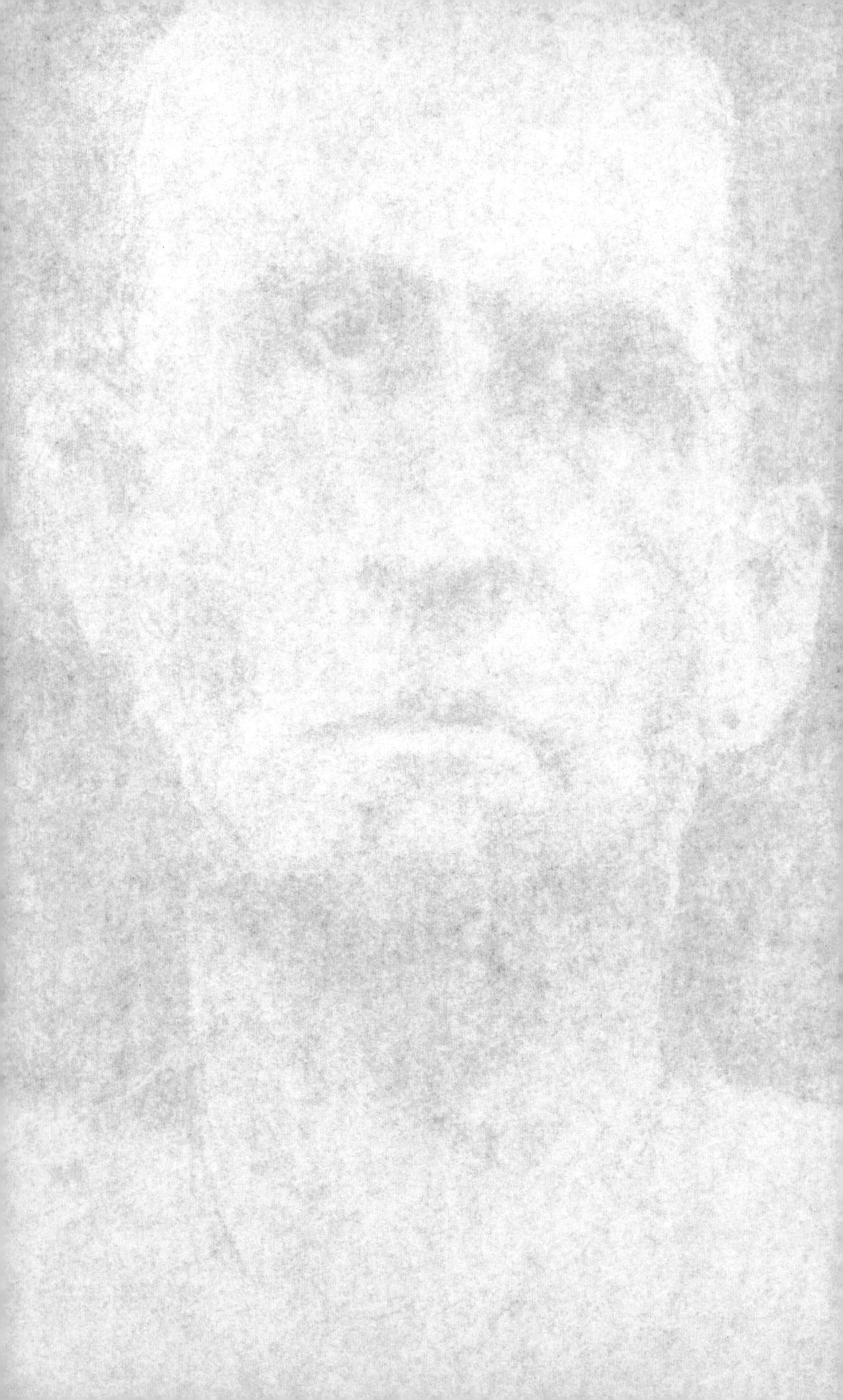

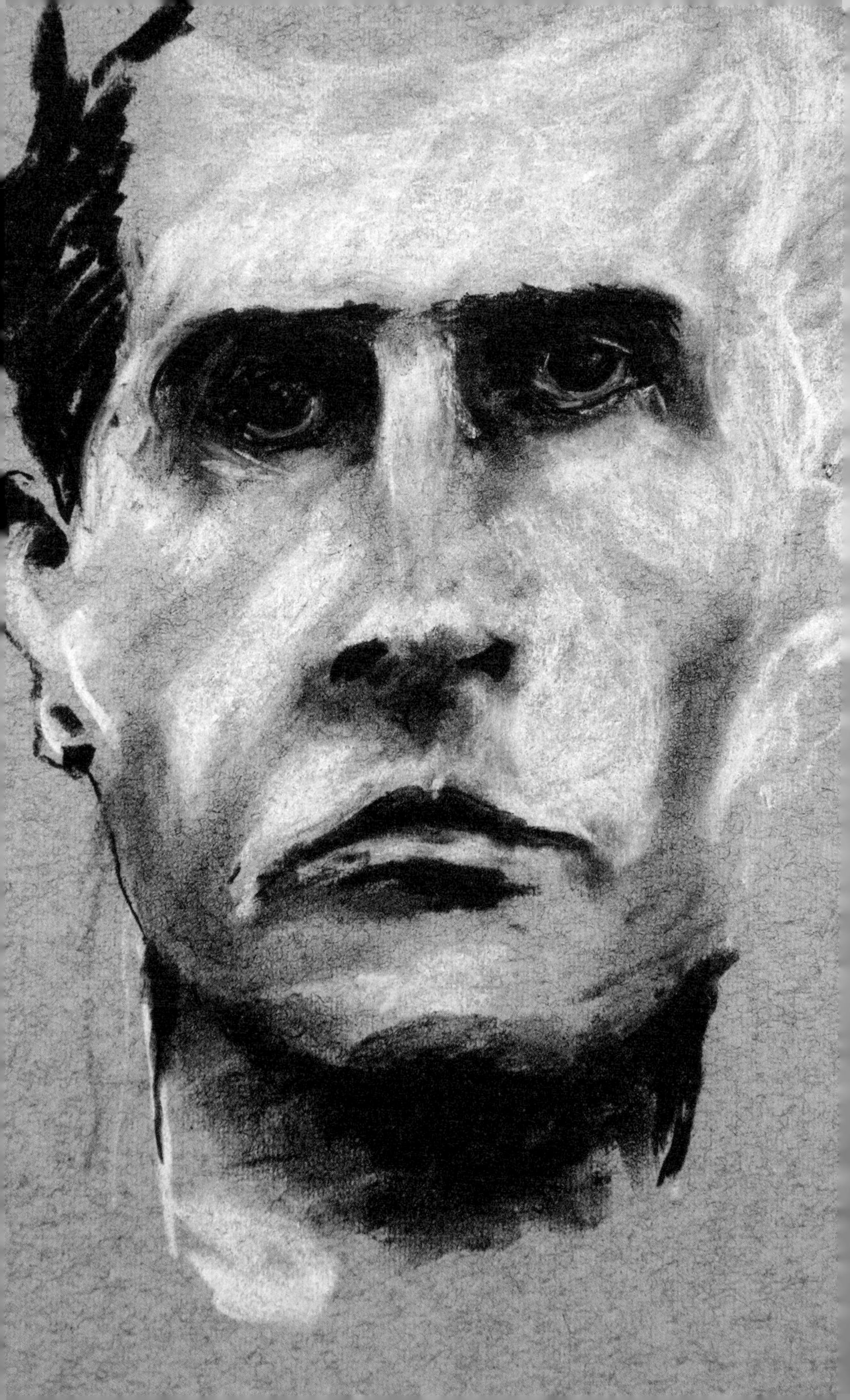

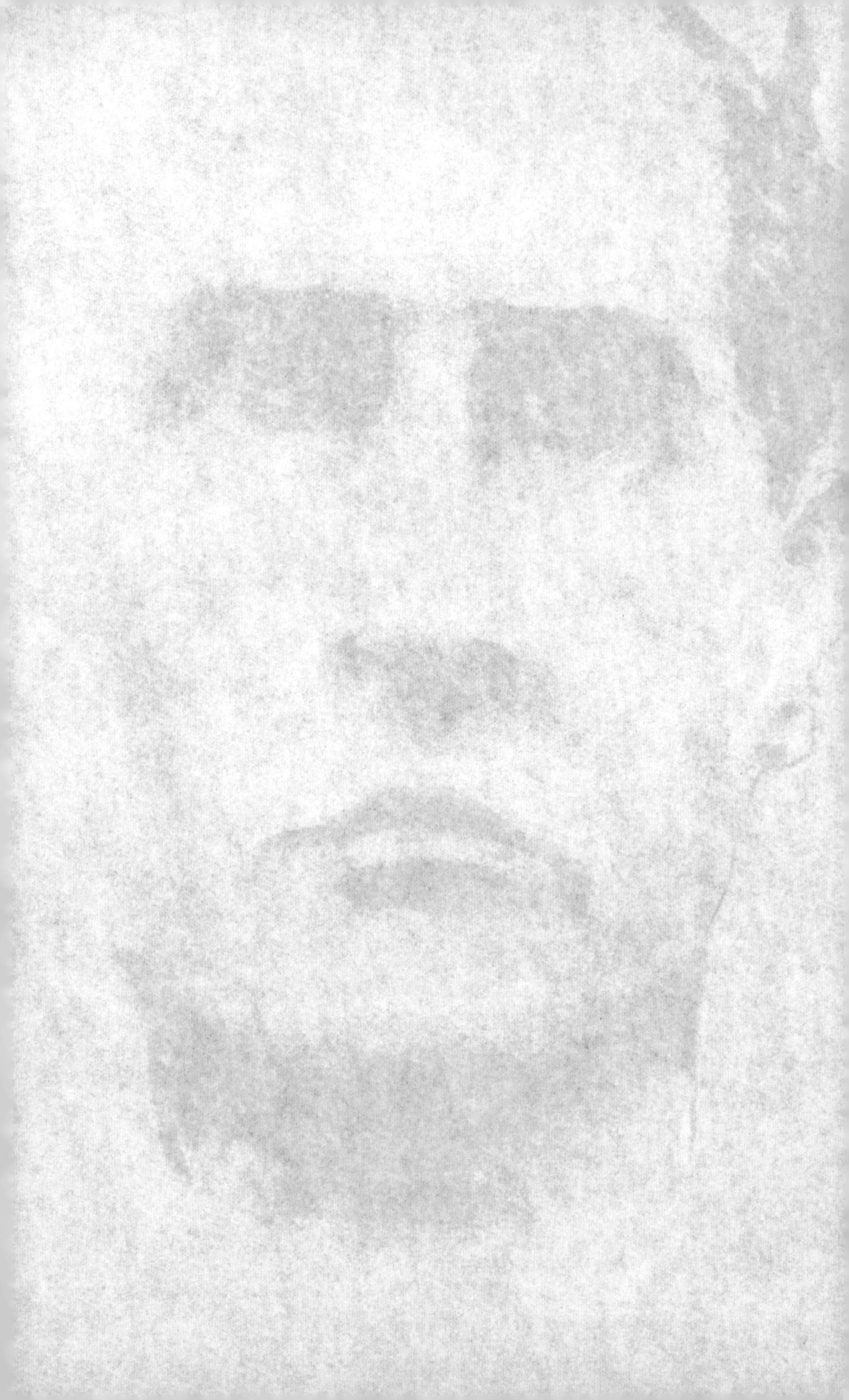

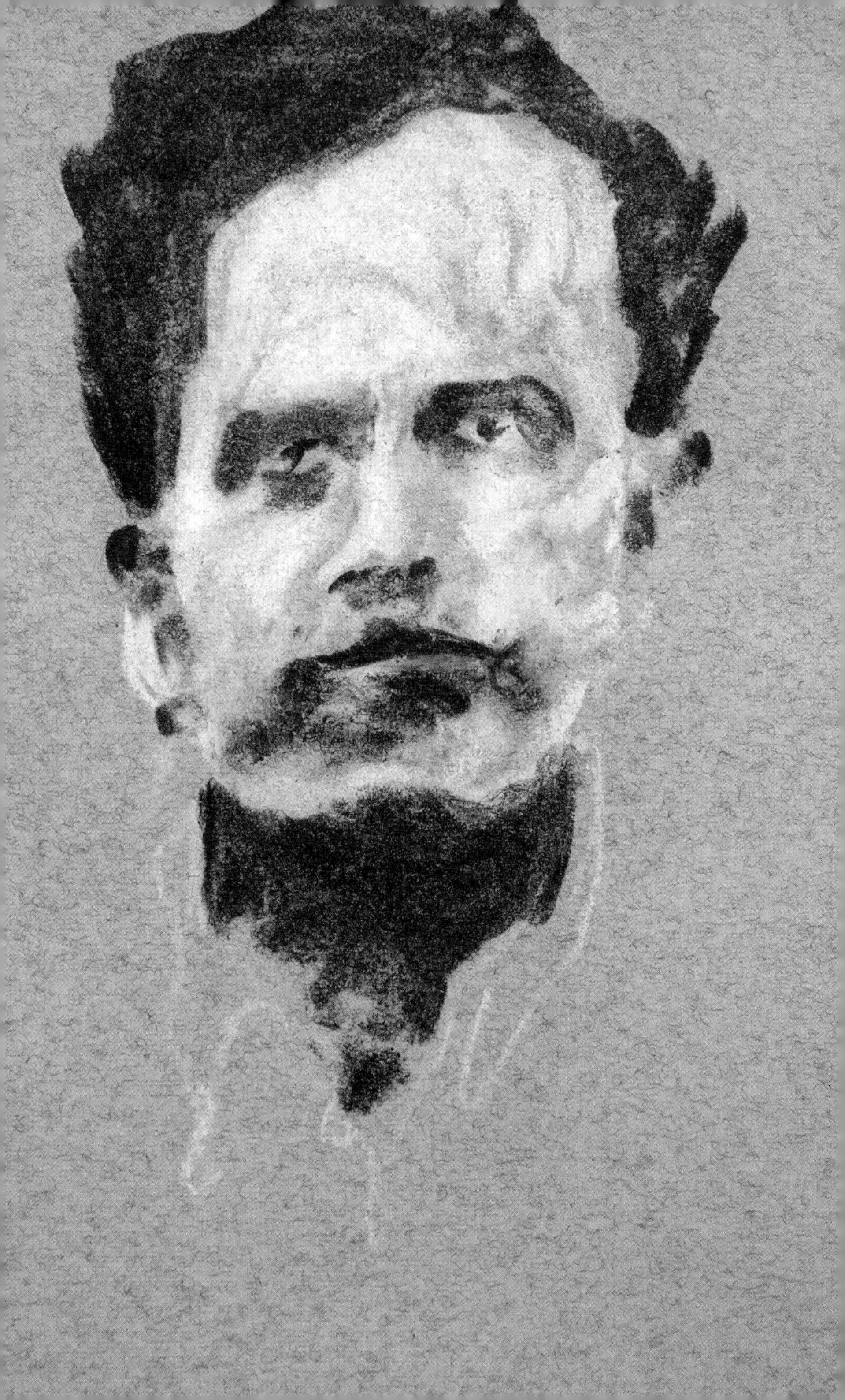

VI:

The Woman of the Galleries

Wittgenstein's Mistress: the very title seems an oxymoron. Women and Wittgenstein in the same sentence? A long, drawn-out sentence, perhaps, with few words and much space between them.

Or a paragraph. David Markson's novel is made of paragraphs, very short ones. Each is both complete, and incomplete. In their incompleteness they are complete. In their consistency they create room for doubt.

There were few women who figured prominently in W's life. Sisters. Student Elizabeth Anscombe, one possible but unrequited love (though he did sometimes call her "old man"). Strangely enough, he did *notice* women. He wrote emphatically in letters of the few that floored him. He was not a virgin, though many thought he was. If there was a mistress, though, she remains a mystery.

One of W's stranger comments was on a particular sculpture that his friend Michael Drobil was working on in 1925. W was quite concerned that the exact proportions might be violated:

> I hope that Drobil has not spoilt anything by enlarging the breast!!! The highly concave breast was *necessary*. It is *quite* easily possible that he has done something stupid! It so happens that the breasts and upper arms should not together form four equal shaped swellings which subsequently, taken as a whole, become an undulating oblique stage before which the rest takes place.... That the breast was not all right is correct, but it is more than likely it cannot be cor-

rected by enlarging it and Drobil himself has, as you will recall, told me in your presence that he will *not* at any rate show the breast *in public. I believe it is not that simple.*[64]

Perhaps Wittgenstein did have a sense of humor. Strange, how this passage sounds more like it was lifted from a fictional account of W than the real thing. The concern with precision, the need for perfection without compromise, the strange choices for emphasis. The exactness of the woman's likeness is what matters, not any sense of emotion that might be conveyed. With a sculpture, exactness can be molded, not sought out of the imperfections of human contact.

On a trip to Norway W remarked uncharacteristically to Drury upon a woman he admired: "A woman who had said to him how fond she was of rats! 'They had such wonderful eyes.' This same woman once sat up every night for a month waiting for a sow to farrow, so as to be on hand to help if necessary."[65] This conviction, this unabashed sense of purpose, would impress Wittgenstein in a woman. In anyone.

But he did not seek out any woman who could be called his equal, in either severity or obsessiveness. She would not be someone who would copy his manners and motives, heaven forbid! Or who would follow him where he wished to go, like the many young men who fell under his sway. No—this woman would have to inhabit W's method, learn his tricks, explore his intellectual haunts, only to make a way through them that would be her own, unmistakable and unique. A formidable character, someone not to be missed. (If, in fact, she was ever there at all.)

This is the character dreamed up by Markson in his novel *Wittgenstein's Mistress*. This book is an assemblage of short paragraphs, one after another, many of them single sentences, with no division into chapters or sections. Space between the sentences is required, for this is no Bernhardian surge where the words must topple over and around each other like the water in a falls. These are pieces of a life, memories of a world that each need to breathe because they suggest so much that has been lost.

This woman is alone, and she seems to exist in a future in which our world has been emptied. She travels the globe, living in art museums. There are no other people alive, for it must be a few years past the apocalypse. Yet the artifacts remain, and she seems to be able to find food wherever she goes. Her work is to try to remember all the names and qualities of the people that are no more. There is no explanation for why she has survived. But it seems she is the last person alive on earth.

Or perhaps she is mad. And she only *sees* the world in this way. This is how reality *appears* to her. And the rest of us see something else entirely.

Each sentence is a mark of something she manages to remember. (*She* has no name—or perhaps she is named Kate? The name is mentioned only once, in passing, like a tiny clue.) Are these memories important? Thrust out of context, alone among its monuments, imagine if you had to stand for all of our culture. It would then be just the way you see it, your own memories, the peculiar bits of information, inexplicable facts, that your mind holds and you cannot shake. You too might be compelled to write it all down.

Other contemporary works also stress the urge to write down all that is known:

An old man in Max Frisch's *Man in the Holocene* knows his mind to be dying, so he writes down all that he knows and tacks it to the wall, making his home an encyclopedia of his memories. Soon the walls are all that he knows. His last certainty: "Today is Tuesday."[66]

Chris Marker's film *La Jetée* takes place in the future, as troglodyte humanity is trying to reconstruct its past by sending a time traveler back into the only scene he can remember from before the Final War. It is: a woman standing alone on a jetty. The film is composed entirely of still photographs, and the time traveler strives to complete a vision of the past through their invocation. If he succeeds, humanity is saved. The only motion in the film is the slow blink of the woman's eyes. Shown this way as a rare technological privilege, it resonates long inside us, impossible to forget, somehow proving that the recollection is real.

But the future, as Marker's character intones, is more protected than the past.[67]

Wittgenstein's Mistress sounds as if it could be excruciating to read but in fact it is impossible to put down. Here is a character who believes that everything she thinks of is worth noting, and must be recorded. For she is the only one left, the last hope for the human race. Her memories become the last gasp of all our memories.

She moves, somehow, traveling across the world. This is not explained. Presumably the machines of locomotion still function and can be commanded by a lone survivor. Planes, trains, boats? In any case, images in the galleries are excellent for the sparking of memories:

> I am quite certain that I lived at the Tate.
> There is an explanation for this, too. The explanation being that one can see the river from there.
> Living alone, one is apt to prefer a view of water.
> I have always admired Turner as well, however. In fact his own paintings of water may well have been a part of what led me to my decision.
> Once, Turner had himself lashed to the mast of a ship for several hours, during a furious storm, so that he could later paint the storm.
> Obviously, it was not the storm itself that Turner intended to paint. What he intended to paint was a representation of the storm.
> One's language is frequently imprecise in that manner, I have discovered.[68]

This last woman chooses to live in a room full of captured images. The artist bound himself to the danger at the thunderous heart of his subject. The philosopher in her wonders how to say exactly what has happened. As she can barely remember it, as the weight of the world's past falls all on her, the last one alive to bear witness.

And she goes on, content, solitary but enjoying life. At times she tears the paintings out of their frames and builds a fire out of the slats. To keep warm. Taking care not to damage the works. But the needs of shelter come first even in the final days of art.

The tone here has been borrowed from Wittgenstein, wrenched out of the old frame of inquiry and intractable work. Trying hard to say what needs be said. Accepting that language is not set up to do the job. Just as no one is *born* to become the last woman alive.

Philosophy is known for seeking questions for which it may seem impossible to find an answer. But the fair mistress knows there is more that could be asked. And she is wont to make statements like this, which might pique the interest even of Wittgenstein: "Evidently not every question falls into the category of questions that would appear to remain unanswerable, however."[69] And yet most of her questions are musings about her own memory, a search for what really happened, for data that no one can possibly corroborate if it is true she is the last human on earth. The very fact that she survives to ask seems preposterous, and she offers no information that dares to explain how she became so fortunate, so singled out.

She wants to remember everything. She retains much information. The kind of question she asks (for this is no *Book of Questions*) is still the impervious kind: She wants to know why one thought follows another. She searches for the route of the train between stations of ideas.

Bricolage—Levi-Strauss' old word for the rag-tag, jumbly way we put together lives in a world overrun with facts and possibilities. Levi-Strauss may have been writing about 'savages,' but all the world is now a grab bag, a yard sale, a flea market of old things that can never be made new without the society to uphold them. It's all junk, it's all rusting memory, and neither the center nor the edges hold. One thought after another. They all have come from somewhere. In her head she hears the old French word one morning, and cannot remember what it means or where she came across it. And then, also, this phrase:

The world is everything that is the case.

The beginning of the *Tractatus*, W's second most famous sentence. It says either nothing, or all that can be said. The mistress—for convenience, let's call her Kate—is writing down everything that is the world for her. She is searching for connections, and the connections she finds will compose the world. There is no one around to verify or falsify the ground of memories. The perfect clean slate for speculation—or composition.

Kate is an artist. She has lived in Soho. Now she can hang her own paintings in the deserted Metropolitan Museum of Art. (Why not?) She refers to artists constantly. They are as alive to her now as her friends and family once were. Sometimes she is living on a beach. Dwelling in a house but taking it apart board by board, feeding the wood to the fire to stay warm. This is the house of memories she takes apart. Sometimes she is living in a museum, burning the frames of canvases to stay warm. At the end she may recall nothing but we hope that she will be at peace.

She remembers that Robert Rauschenberg once erased a drawing of Willem de Kooning and called it *Erased de Kooning Drawing*. She knows at the end that her house will "look as if Robert Rauschenberg had gotten to it."[70]

We are terrified of erasing our own words. Composed with technology, they are rarely safe. They could disappear in a second, vaporized by the crash of a disk, a ghost in the machine. Memories may be more secure, at least for a time.

They are unique in the particular links they follow, in the ecology of facts we can each string from the discontinuities of what we hold inside. For example, the way Kate arrives at W, charting an improbable path, sewing an irregular stitch in the seamless cloth of possibility.

She remembers having once read a children's book on the life of Johannes Brahms. The book notes that Brahms often carried candy in his pockets to give to children at the houses he visited in Vienna. And this remote fact has a link somehow to the one sentence Kate has ever read by W:

> ...come to think about it I once read somewhere that Ludwig Wittgenstein himself had never read one word of Aristotle.
>
> In fact I have more than once taken comfort in knowing this, there being so may people one has never read one word of one's self.
>
> Such as Ludwig Wittgenstein.
>
> Even if one was always told that Wittgenstein was too hard to read in any case.

And to tell the truth I did once read one sentence by him after all, which I did not find difficult in the least. In fact I became very fond of what it said.

You do not need a lot of money to buy a nice present, but you do need a lot of time, was the sentence.

On my honor, Wittgenstein once said that....

Well, and I certainly would have found it agreeable to tell Ludwig Wittgenstein how fond I am of his sentence.[71]

And so too the gift of thought requires time and the slowing of a wanting, incessant pace. Slow down, but still with a purpose in mind.

These are the kind of sentences that W will be most remembered for, along with the famous, sweeping, and bleak pronouncements that want to explain everything by announcing what can and can't be explained. And where did he get the idea? Well, says Kate, think back to his childhood. One doesn't have to have read any words of W to remember the strange details of his past. Everyone knows that Brahms used to come calling at the family home on the Alleegasse! So it is likely (an insight!) that young W was one of the children who got candy from the old master:

Very possibly this was what was in Wittgenstein's own mind all of those years later, in fact, when he said that you do not need a lot of money to give a nice present, but you do need a lot of time.

By which I mean that if the person Wittgenstein

had wished to give a present to had been a child, he could have naturally taken care of the problem exactly the way Brahms generally did.

Doubtless one does not stroll about Cambridge carrying candy in one's pocket to give to Bertrand Russell or to Alfred North Whitehead, however.

Although what one might now wish one's self is that Wittgenstein had been in the basement with me yesterday, so as to have given me some help with that *Dasein*.

Well, or perhaps even with that other word, *bricolage*, that I woke up with in my head, that morning.[72]

So you see how her mind is working. It works on itself. There are no outside human stimuli. She can give no one a present but herself. She learns to generalize by saying "one" instead of "I." This is a plea to make the discoveries not about the personality but about the world.

W tried to forget who he was to serve openly the truth. Kate knows that the answer for why she thinks what she thinks will only be found in the truth of her own past. (*Isn't it just like a woman?*—Can we still say things like that?)

She philosophizes through the asides of others' thoughts. Not the core of the argument, but phrases left at the fringes. These may often be the most memorable. You can tell a lot about a person by what they remark off the cuff, when they seem to be off guard. Some of this trivia sounds preposterous: "Martin Heidegger once owned a pair of boots that had actually belonged to Vincent van Gogh, and used to put them on when he went for walks in the woods.... What he surely would have admired about Van Gogh to begin with would have been the way Van Gogh could make even a pair of boots seem to have anxiety in them."[73]

W used to think so hard you could see him doing it, she remembers. And wonders what that would be like. We see Kate thinking because we are reading the inner course of her thoughts. One thing is recalled, and then another, so far away. What insight binds them? This is how poetry starts, and at its most crisp becomes poetic philosophy. It fails when it ends up too cold.

The whole enterprise may be too cold. That's when I want to give up: when I find myself obsessed with a person who became so wrapped up in unanswerables that he could not see how far he was from the wonder of the world. And that wonder is what might make philosophy optimistic, to fight its tendency to criticize and to shoot down all who believe and cannot explain why.

How to be happy in the face of such unsettlement? Think of the beauty of the words themselves, and the way they open up doors to further discovery. If we are to throw away the ladder once we get there, where have we ascended to? There are so many ladders, so many stories to inhabit, cliffs to climb over. The climber does not climb the rope, but uses it for safety as she touches the rock with her bare hands. Philosophy is a form of precaution. Don't throw it away. You will need it for the next pitch. Each satisfaction is a ledge, not a summit. There is no peak at the end of this climb.

We see Kate thinking because we are literally reading her thoughts, observing her hunt for connections. These links are tenuous at best, like the bonds between synapses firing in all of us. We *see* her searching for unity, trying to spread her mind around all that is the case, to reassure herself that it *is* there that she has a place, that she is alive to document it.

Has this woman been thrust into unforeseen circumstances, or has she found what we all find when we dare to look inside? This is the final question, the one that arises toward the end of this novel that seems impossible to end because it takes place in a time beyond the end of time. Group time. Social time. The time of witness, from one person to another. This is the last gasp of time. And she struggles to hold on to what will eventually be lost. Like all of us. Unless we leave some legacy, some trace.

Of course she comes to the inevitable question: Was she this much alone before all the unhinging happened? And she will come to blame her predicament as much upon essence as on event:

> One manner of being alone simply being different from another manner of being alone, being all that she would finally decide that this came down to, as well.
>
> Which is to say that even when one's telephone still does function one can be as alone as when it does not.
>
> Or that even when one still does hear one's name being called at certain intersections one can be as alone as when one is only able to imagine that this has happened.

So that quite possibly the whole point of the novel might be that one can just as easily ask for Modigliani on a telephone that does not function as on one that does.[74]

The condition of the tool does not change your distance from what is no more. You may fix the machine but there still is no one else but you. Once there was, though, and the question remains: did you appreciate them while they were there? Did they need you? Would they miss you if only you were gone and not the rest of the human race?

Is it the loneliness or the madness that brings on such independence? The equal distance between ideas is the sadness of open space, or the solace of resignation. There will be no one else. Or as W said on his final birthday: "There will be no more returns."[75]

The author of a book like this "would not be able to keep out of my heroine's head after all."[76] There is nothing but the inside of her head for the mine of memories. Outside, the remains of empty civilization only decay. The report inside the head is not a plot, it is not a system, it is not a rant or a stream of consciousness. It is like a chain of ideas, where the links float apart and reconnect, shuffling among themselves, all pointing to some order that can never be expressed. Here's how it ends, suddenly shorthand, instantly a poem:

Once, I had a dream of fame.
Generally, even then, I was lonely.
To the castle, a sign must have said.
Somebody is living on this beach.[77]

Following directions to the castle, I am suddenly a Kafka character named K, adrift on quest to challenge authority. Wanting to stand out pushes the crowd away. The shoreline is the end of one world and the beginning of another.

theoretical need of atomic propositions and simple terms or na[mes]
from the formal requirements for determinateness of sense a

[...]ty]

[com]posite proposition is a function of its constituent proposit[ions]
[c]an have sense only if these have sense. Finally we must ge[t]
[ato]mic propositions whose sense must be determined not by
[fur]ther reduction to other propositions but by direct referenc[e]
facts in the world. And an atomic proposition in its turn
[i]s to have sense must be constituted of primitive term[s]
[na]mes with fixed meanings in our experience, i.e. terms wh[ich]
[a]re not defined by other terms, but which stand as signals fo[r]
[im]mediate elements within our experience. Otherwise we
[coul]d analyse the propositions in which they occur into
[pro]duct of other propositions and the atomicity of the
[orig]inal proposition would not be real Thus if we are
[to ha]ve sensible atomic prop^{ns} we must have simple terms
[....]

[If our lang. is to be significant in the world there must be
[simp]le elts. or obj's which we could name &, atomic facts wh[ich]
[(if there is a world) (i.e. in world)]
[woul]d denote &(& which make some of the atomic prop^{ns} true)

[Thm]: To have sensible (composite) propositions, must have
[sensi]ble atomic propositions.
[mo]re "   "   "   "   must have simple terms or nam[es]
[&] "   "   "   "
simple elts. or obj's named)

[Note]: this line of arg. seems to suggest the wld. is the totality of things,
[not] of facts)

[Fund]'l princ. of positivism is. Each prop^n in a perf. lang. must have one fixed def-
[inite] meth. of verification; if a prop^n has several senses then we have not yet b[ut]
[an in]cludis expressed by the same prop'l sign. If the sense of the prop^n is in[definite we]
have no definite prop^n & we ought to determine the precise sense. Definiteness [(or ambiguity)]

[Return] of Wd. discussion of names: Names must possess 2 char^s: (A) th[ey]
[...]his in relation to our lang. i.e. not further definable in our symbo[lism]
[&] to stand as symbols for s.th. definite & unique in the wld., i.e. th[ey]
[have] definite meaning)
[We], if in our lang. in order to be significant, must have simple undefinable
[sig]n[s], for diff. elts. in our wld. (cf. 32 a)
[B] a name is a primitive sign relative to our language;
[i.e.] as the end of our definitions, established by ostensive def.
[...] end of our names are simple. But note that the simples

VII:

The Possibility of Reddish Green

Wittgenstein denied the existence of reddish green, a color on a continuum between red and green. That's not the way we see, that's not the way we name, he said. But in philosophy, as in art, "we must always be prepared to learn something totally new."[78]

The possibility of reddish green is the image of hope guiding this book. That if seeing is always seeing from somewhere, there is always another way to see. In autumn the red and green are all around us, and in between is the reddish green of human possibility, allowing us to dream that there is always a completely different way to see things, if we can strip our preconceptions bare.

So we may learn how to live between the red and the green. Colors may come before words. And by claiming that reddish green, or greenish red, is impossible, W may very well be demanding that we seek to prove the opposite of what he says.

"What, no reddish green!" cries an artist I know, as I explain there once was a man who doubted it. "I have seen it."

And orange blue? Yellow violet? These creations are challenges for perception to look beyond its first level.

A hundred and forty years earlier, Goethe too had an unconventional theory of color, beautifully written, and challenging the conventions of science as Wittgenstein challenges the conventions of perception.[79] But apart from their different notions of where to look for the concept of color, Goethe and Wittgenstein are talking about the same thing.

> We never sufficiently reflect that a language, strictly speaking, can only be symbolical and figurative, that it can never express things directly, but only, as it were, reflectedly. (Goethe)[80]

> But what kind of proposition is that, that blending in white removes the coloredness from the color?... Here the temptation to believe in a phenomenology, something midway between science and logic, is very great. (Wittgenstein)[81]

And there is a sense in which, upon seeing the same things, they wish to draw different conclusions.

> If, however, a writer could use all these modes of description and...give forth the result of his observations in a diversified language.... Yet, how difficult it is to avoid substituting the sign for the thing; how difficult to keep the essential quality still living before us, and not to kill it with the word.[82]

> In philosophy, [one learns] how to speak about [a subject].... The rule-governed nature of languages permeates our life.[83]

For Goethe, languages have the unfortunate tendency to destroy phenomena through analysis, while Wittgenstein implies that languages are all that exists for us. He speaks of them largely by revealing their self-contradictions.

So Wittgenstein's colors are linguistic expressions, whose consistency in various uses is to be tested. Goethe's are captured revelations of the inspiring and expiring of nature.

Compare their respective depictions of specific sensations of color in perceived situations:

> I had entered an inn towards evening, and, as a well-favored girl, with a brilliantly fair complexion, black hair, and a scarlet bodice, came into the room, I looked attentively at her as she stood before me at some distance in half shadow. As she presently afterward turned away, I saw on the white wall, which was now before me, a black face surrounded with a bright light, while the dress of the perfectly distinct figure appeared a beautiful sea-green.[84]

> I saw in a [black-and-white] photograph a boy with slicked-back blond hair and a dirty light-colored jacket, and a man with dark hair, standing in front of a machine .... The finished iron parts were iron colored, the boy's hair was blond, the castings black, the grating zinc-colored, despite the fact that everything was depicted simply in lighter and darker shades of the photographic paper.[85]

Wittgenstein inspects an image in black and white, and asks: why do I see colors in it within these simply light and dark shadows? Goethe looks at a woman in bright clothing and notes how her image, in reverse, remains after she moves away. He sees a real image in color, and observes how its absence creates a virtual image that suggests the great fluxing of light and dark. (Of course they are also seeing boys and girls, and must think of many more things beyond the surface and the picture.)

Wittgenstein is asking: what are black and white that they can contain so much? Goethe asks: what are colors that they can reveal the lightening and darkening of nature?

Even now I am puzzled by Wittgenstein's willingness to be trapped in language. He fails to see its potential to free us, to bring us to places which phenomena alone cannot. He says: our languages are governed by rules; but he does not say: these rules lead to consequences which our perceptions do not.

He asks: Can there be reddish green? Can there be transparent white? He answers no, showing that colors cannot be combined as easily as words referring to color can be. In doing so, he misses the power of the language game. The power is: when we *say* "reddish green," when we *say* "transparent white," *images are evoked* in us.

I see these supposed contradictions all around me—the glass is both half empty and half full. Perception demands memory to get a hold on us. The city is beautifully energetic or a monument to social decay. A single glance can grasp it as both.

Scientists have worked hard on the problem of how to see reddish green. They have presented observers with alternately sharp and blurry strips of the two colors, tricking the eyes into seeing the boundary between the two hues disappear. Some of the subjects could see the mythical color, a place nowhere on the spectrum at all. Their conclusion: "Working with limited information coming in through its sense channels the brain can persuade itself that such a color exists. There is more going on here than meets the eye."[86]

Perhaps not being red is part of being green.

To understand what reddish green would mean, says W, we should need to be able to present a continuum between the colors red and green. But that is only one theory about how two colors can be related: look at a stand of autumn swamp maple trees. Some can be red. Some can be green. Would it be correct to say that, as we move away from the stand of trees, the color we perceive tends to unify towards reddish green?

And if we look at a single leaf, one in the process of changing—what do we call the color at the point where the green leaf is gradually turning to red? The color could not be brown, as Wittgenstein implies, for that is the color the leaves turn to only after turning from green to red.

Is it possible that the changes of color on a single leaf mirror the changes we observe as we step back from the changing grove of trees? In other words: could some cells of the leaf be green, and nearby cells red, so that at a distance of a few inches we observe the whole area as being a single intermediate color? This would be a type of observation of which Goethe would approve.

> True observers of nature ... will agree that all which presents itself as appearance, all that we meet with as phenomenon, must either indicate an original division which is capable of union, or

an original unity which admits of division, and that the phenomenon will present itself accordingly. To divide the united, to unite the divided, is the life of nature; this is the eternal systole and diastole, the eternal collapsion and expansion, the inspiration and expiration of the world in which we live and move.[87]

Breathing in, breathing out—nature is only separable into unities and diversities in its ability to combine and divide again into new patterns.

The painter Georges Seurat knew about this, and was able to create luminescent grays that glow vibrantly precisely because he knew how to place adjacent areas of red and green so that, if we stand back a certain distance from the painting, there is a point where the colors are caught between cancelling each other out and starting some kind of fireworks. In the case of his painting *Les Poseuses,* one must stand about six feet back to see it.[88]

For Goethe, the persistent problem in the description of this process is the tendency of specific languages to overcome the potential of change, to fix nature in lifeless words, to replace things with their names. For Goethe there *is* a life beyond any particular language. And this life is something we can describe, if we diversify language itself through the acceptance of different kinds of descriptions at once— bringing them together, breaking them into parts, but always moving.

When darkness is presented to the eye it demands brightness, and vice versa: it shows its vital energy, its fitness to receive the impression of the object, precisely by spontaneously tending to an opposite state.[89]

Thus the living presence of the dark-haired woman reverses itself to its negative image on the wall. In which form, as memory or image, does it remain in Goethe's mind?

Someone who agrees with Goethe believes that Goethe correctly recognized the nature of color. And nature here is not what results from experiments, but it lies in the concept of color… It would also be wrong to say "Just look at the colors in nature and you will see that it is so." For looking does not teach us anything about the concepts of colors.[90]

Goethe would have to disagree, for he thought the very breath of nature was visible and present in the *Urphänomen* of color: that lightness and dark were primal phenomena behind our concept of color. But Wittgenstein says that this, too, is a concept. He says that we only learn about colors in the way we use them. And for him, this is revealed in the way we *talk* about using them.

And this is why he is confused by the expression "transparent white." Goethe considers white to be an opaque color, so he would not even talk about its transparency. Wittgenstein notes the linguistic puzzle. We will see how transparent white evokes plural interpretations, and thus cannot be dismissed in either manner.

A transparent color: a color which we can see through. Everything behind the transparency *takes on the character* of the transparent color.

So everything behind green glasses *appears* green? Yes, but in practice, in use, we can distinguish some colors behind any monochromatic glass. Jonathan Westphal claims that a white surface seen under blue light "does not look blue. It looks white."[91] I say: it looks blue, but with certain *characteristics* of white: dazzling, brightest of colors, furthest away from absolute darkness, in this case—darkest blue.

The notion of transparency applied to white could have several meanings, as there are several characteristics of white that everything behind the transparency could take on. **Dazzling**: all colors behind the glass could be more intense, brighter, more fluorescent than before. **Absoluteness**: a transparent white might remove variation between colors and produce a *high contrast* image; only black, only white, pure brightness and pure darkness. Or, **Whitening**: in the way transparent green makes things greener, but still identifiable, transparent white could make all imagery lighter, fainter, closer to white, while retaining some qualities of its original color.

We find an ambiguity in the words light and bright, dark and black, which might have amused Wittgenstein. He could also say: a glass could not do the things you have described.

But he did not see the relevance of postulating a notion of transparency distant from that which we normally use. He started to suggest a cinema screen on which a black-and-white film is projected as an analogy to transparent white, but rejected it on the grounds that we do not speak of such a screen in this way.

The three approaches to transparency for white listed above might be appropriate in an electronic environment—where color as it is to be perceived by us becomes something to be synthesized artificially. Transparency becomes an operation which can be performed on any color.

How would Wittgenstein or Goethe have reacted to today's digital, pointillistic treatment of color? Perhaps we now see color differently, detached from primal, natural light and dark. If so—and if we are sufficiently open to the possibility of languages consistent in a way that machines can understand—might we perhaps place less weight on the intuition that 'transparent' and 'white' do not go together? For example: if we tell a computer to apply function f to color C, who's to stop us from permitting $f(C)$ where $C =$ white? How could we program the computer to deal with this information? By turning any of our three approaches listed above into an algorithm for operating upon the information that constitutes the image.

Goethe, if presented with the question of technology's effect on our perception of color, might critique these views of "operative transparency of white" by submitting them to the criteria of symbolic use, remembering that only "a use that fully harmonizes with nature could be called symbolic"—in the words of Klaus Meyer-Abich, who goes on to conclude that, for Goethe, "art and technology must follow the same path." [92] They must refer back to an original identity present in nature. Now could the juxtaposition of 'transparency' and 'white' ever be natural in this manner? (Is Goethe merely arguing for the primacy of one language game over all others?)

> There is no such thing as phenomenology, but there are indeed phenomenological problems. [93]

Wittgenstein, like Schiller, wants to call Goethe's apprehending of the primal light and dark in nature "an idea, not an empirical experience." To Schiller, Goethe retorted, "How grand that I have ideas without knowing it, and can see them with my very eyes." Yet he knew that it was possible, even then, for others to refute his observations on the grounds that they were theory-laden, as well as emotion-laden in their harsh views of Newton. Goethe knew his own theory offered not merely a language, but a goal towards which multiple languages could strive in their attempt to describe. This could not stand up as a critique of Newton, though, as the latter was enjoying so much success through scientific confirmation of his theories.

Goethe tried to describe colors as we see them, not as ideal forms required by language. Wittgenstein implies that pure white is derived from observed, imperfect whites in the same way we construct a geometry. The ideal white means white "carried to extremes—which can teach us something about its actual use."

And Goethe should say: why carry white to its extremes, when the interplay of darkness and light in its fullness is present to the observer who learns *to see*? And yet his *reason* for learning to see is similar again to Wittgenstein's:

> The investigator of nature cannot be required to be a philosopher, but it is expected that he should so far have attained the habit of philosophizing, as to distinguish himself essentially from the world, in order to associate himself with it again in a higher sense.[94]

The trap of the philosopher, scientist, or anyone who seeks knowledge is to set up a method of inquiry that cannot reach the truth.

> Hence arises an endless confusion, a mere verbiage, a constant endeavor to seek and to find subterfuges whenever truth presents itself and threatens to be overpowering.[95]

Wittgenstein, on the other hand, does not claim to seek truth, but to be pragmatic:

> What I actually want to say is that here too it is not a matter of the words one uses or of what one is thinking when using them, but rather of the differences they make at various points in life.[96]

This is the ultimate criterion: *Our* questions, *our* thinking, must be taken as the most serious thing. Defining all these color terms does not matter until it actually changes our lives.

> When someone who believes in God looks around him
> and asks "Where did everything that I see come from?"
> … he is expressing an attitude toward all explanations.—
> But how is this shown in his life? It is the attitude that
> takes a particular matter seriously, but then at a partic-
> ular point doesn't take it seriously after all, and declares
> that something else is even more serious.[97]

What must one believe in to be able to take Goethe's theory of color seriously? Nature looks back at us. There is
life in nature that speaks to us, that shows itself to us, with
rhythm, contrast, and shadow. One does not need a God to
accept his system, but one must believe that there is something to be seen outside of use and function. Of course
such a theory could never be proved wrong, because it is a
belief, and one with a practical objective: to teach a way of
attentiveness, not just to languages, but to changes in the
world that clearly existed long before mankind was able to
cognize them.

> Like a giant tower
> The fog-girded oak,
> From the bushes peers darkness
> With a hundred black glances.[98]

In this early poem, Goethe's nature looks back, with a
blackness that must, by necessity, contain the possibility of
light—and thus of all the colors in between.

Contrary to both Wittgenstein and Goethe, this morning I
awoke to see a dazzling *gray* sky outside through the transparent window. It was brighter than the clarity of blue and

more present than the predictable intensity of night. But maybe it, too, contains that well-known extreme—possibility.

Or: the hope that there is more to the world than is first seen or explained. If we are lucky, some phrase of this record may open up a new way of organizing the world as it appears. Look not at the file of people walking down the waterside sidewalk in their coats of red and green, but at the spaces in between all that you see. That gap between two nearby trees that forms a tall thin sliver of a triangle of space: try organizing the world around that. Inside, there is a space no one cares to notice. And from such a perspective a world of betweenthings may emerge.

The philosophy that lets the dance of the world be joined from a new angle will be the one that sings.

VIII:

A Picture Held Us Captive

1995, San Francisco

Doug Hall: What I am trying to say is that while it may be true that the Philosophical Investigations *challenges central arguments in the* Tractatus—*in fact I don't feel that I know enough to make that assertion—what interests me is that within the* Tractatus *itself there are contradicting statements that cancel out whatever logical argumentation there may be, making the entire enterprise nonsense. And I mean nonsense in the way I understand W uses the term, as meaning those experiences that fall beyond the logical constraints of language and what can be known through language. In that way it seems to me that the book is closer to poetry than it is to analytic philosophy.*

DR: It certainly does at the end.

Doug Hall: Yes. And earlier. You begin to notice slippages where he starts saying things like "What can be shown cannot be said," and "Whatever we can describe could be other than what it is," or "Language disguises thought."

DR: Well, there is this whole idea, it is all here in the end, where it's suggesting that what is really important are all those things that he never talked about...

Doug Hall: Yes.

DR: ...that the entire book could be wrong.

Doug Hall: Yes. Philosophically wrong. I guess. But perhaps, like Finnegans Wake, *not poetically wrong.*

DR: ....that the whole book could just be this game...

Doug Hall: Yes.

DR: That, that...

Doug Hall: There's a statement that I came across some-where. I don't know if it is in the Tractatus *or maybe in the* Blue *or the* Brown *notebooks, where he says something like, "We are taught to play a game according to the rules, but the rules can be changed at any time, and what we presumed to know about the game can prove to be entirely false." This sounds more like John Cage than Bertrand Russell.*

DR: Yes...

Doug Hall: I've always felt that more than anything, the Tractatus *is a sort of a poignant lament to the limitations of language. It's the inability of language to adequately de-scribe the world or at least the world beyond the logic of lan-guage. I think this is the world of experience and feeling and the only one that really matters to us. Using Wittgenstein's logic, this world that's beyond language can only be shown, not captured by conventional language.*

I am speaking here with Doug Hall, an artist based in San Francisco, in two long interviews twenty-one years apart. Wittgenstein has spoken to artists more than any phi-losopher of our time. This is not only because his insights have been presented in the form of moments, waiting to be plucked out for instant meaning. W's key concern with what can be said and what cannot be said can easily be transposed into the realm of art: What can be made, what cannot be made. What can be explained about what is made, what remains in the dark. How much of the creative process can be seen as a game, with its own peculiar rules, and how much of it is a form of play that manages to present what cannot be said, what will never be explained…

Among contemporary artists the name Joseph Kosuth often comes up in reference to the influence of Wittgenstein. Kosuth has created works of art out of quotations from W, with titles from W. On the centennial of W's birth in 1989, he curated a major exhibition, mounted in Vienna and Brussels, of works from many artists celebrating the influence of W (as he saw it) on the art of the twentieth century.[99]

This is the century, says Kosuth, that has marked "the end of philosophy and the beginning of art."[100] It is an arrogant statement, and Kosuth is quick to qualify, denying causal connection.

This is the century, one might say, when so much in our culture seems to break apart, in dissipation or a tremendous crash. Music explores increased chromaticism to the point of denying any tonal center, leading to the stratification of Schoenberg's twelve-tone system. He thought this was the end of harmony in music—in fact it was a gigantic question mark. Paul Klee heralded a new art born of abstraction, built on rules of line and shape that would be as pure as the musical harmonies of the baroque period. Both these characters dreamed of order, but instead they were the harbingers of chaos!

There is no end to human creativity, only endless beginnings. What seemed the finish of art was in fact the start of an art merged with philosophy—a conceptual and performative endeavor where borders begin to fall away. Where a work means nothing without its explanation, where an artist might have a hard time separating himself from what he has made.

This tendency of art to become philosophy means that art includes its own criticism or explanation, in order to make sense of creations that seem unreadable or difficult to know. There can be many dangers in this. Philosophy may not always add to art if the two are combined. More often I believe it would be better if philosophy became more like art, rather than the other way round. We would stop asking endless questions with unsatisfactory answers, and instead try to create something beautiful.

I fear the urge to explain might lessen the power of art. Art works most powerfully when it does not depend on explanation. At the same time, it need never be afraid of the expression of difficult thoughts.

Kosuth says he has "taken the precarious position of predicting that art will replace philosophy."[101] It is in the realm of art that speculation is both possible and unbounded. Anything can be said, anything can be claimed. Thus it is the place for the new.

Joseph Kosuth's work often features words on a wall, sometimes simply quoted, sometimes crossed out, sometimes in many languages. Often he uses the words of Wittgenstein.

By now you should understand why. Just put such words up there and watch how people respond. Is that enough to be art?

He's not the only artist to become enamored of the words of Wittgenstein. Doug Hall has proposed a *Wittgenstein Plaza* to be built on the banks of the Danube in Vienna. The monument would be a flat circle of stone with words engraved in a concentric pattern around the center. The words would be quotations from the *Tractatus*, inscribed in all the various languages that touch the river in its course: German, French, Hungarian, Slovak, Slovenian, Rumanian, Bulgarian, and Russian.

Not that W spoke all these languages, or that his works are necessarily current in all the different tongues. Just that the circle is to be on the banks of the river, and the river wends its way past all these lands to the sea.

And why play with the text this way? Why curve the words of Witgenstein around an unsayable center? Hall explains: "In art there is a lot of talk about how the artist functions as an author that produces images and relationships between images. At a certain point, the artist's authorship stops and the viewer's authorship starts. That is the whole notion of a dynamic text that interacts with our bodies and minds. And that is the lesson of Wittgenstein for me."[102]

You may plan for things to be seen in one way, and then they are seen in another. It is the artist's role to set the stage for the most illuminating possible encounters.

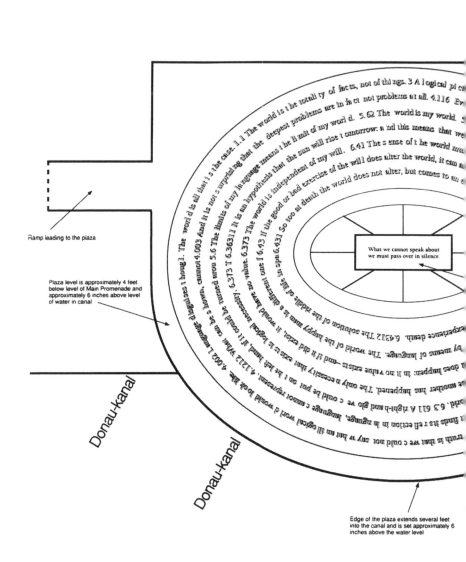

Ramp leading to the plaza

Plaza level is approximately 4 feet below level of Main Promenade and approximately 6 inches above level of water in canal

Donau-kanal

Donau-kanal

Edge of the plaza extends several feet into the canal and is set approximately 6 inches above the water level

What we cannot speak about we must pass over in silence.

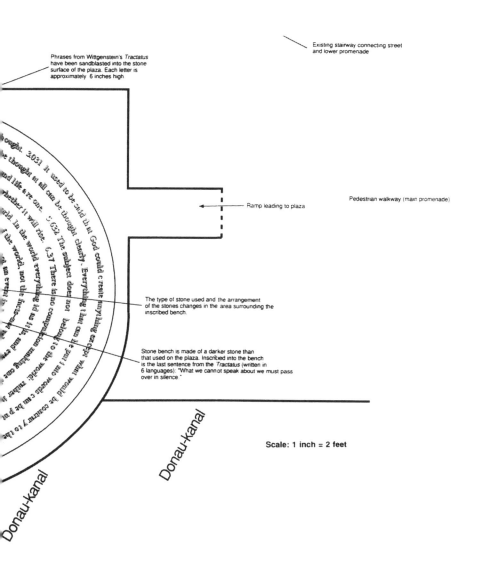

Phrases from Wittgenstein's *Tractatus* have been sandblasted into the stone surface of the plaza. Each letter is approximately 6 inches high

Existing stairway connecting street and lower promenade

Ramp leading to plaza

Pedestrian walkway (main promenade)

The type of stone used and the arrangement of the stones changes in the area surrounding the inscribed bench.

Stone bench is made of a darker stone than that used on the plaza. Inscribed into the bench is the last sentence from the *Tractatus* (written in 6 languages): "What we cannot speak about we must pass over in silence."

Donau-kanal

Donau-kanal

Donau-kanal

Scale: 1 inch = 2 feet

Doug Hall: Vienna in its prime was the gateway between the East and the West. The cultural and political center of the Austro-Hungarian empire. But today the city is like the crowned head of the emperor that has been disconnected from its imperial body. The glitz has been left behind while the substance has vanished. W writes in the Tractatus: *"Whatever we see could be other than what it is." Maybe what Wittgenstein is really talking about is this impossibility of fully understanding things and the dialectic of attempting to understand.*

I am interested in this idea that you would physically move through language, walking right into the middle of it, where the didactic argument is undermined by the very structure of the work, which is clearly an admission of the inability of language to describe the world.

DR: Your proposal depends a lot on words to make its point. Do you think there is a way to make a Wittgenstein plaza that does not depend so much on words?

Doug Hall: I am sure there is. Would it be silence? I think that language can be an image, and I think that the ability of language—phrases, constellations of words, fragments caught out of the corner the eye—to interact with our consciousness is very profound. And I am interested in the dialectic that exists when that happens. I find many of W's aphoristic phrases to be evocative and mysterious, in the way the best poetry can be. I think I could be accused of using his words as a kind of surrogate or stand-in for my own words. Or more exactly, my inability to use my own words poetically. At this moment in my life it's very hard for me to write expressionistically, so I suppose I'm attempting to deflect my emotional inadequacy by usurping the emotions, or the poetic possibilities, that I think underlay W's words.

DR: Ah, then you don't have to take responsibility for it. That is interesting. But there is this sense of coldness there that really troubles me. As in those books by Thomas Bernhard—he wrote not one but two novels about Wittgenstein. They are cold as steel.

Doug Hall: Ouch! Let's take the responsibility issue first. I guess it's true that by using W's words I can claim innocence. It's sort of don't blame me blame W. But I do have to take responsibility for usurping them and for the way they are presented. And for what might be revealed by my appropriation. But what do you mean by cold? Impenetrable, or...?

DR: The emotion, when it is revealed, is so guarded.

Doug Hall: I guess my response is multifold. First, you have to remember that my proposal is in its initial stages, and if it is given the green light for development I will find an architect and begin to develop the project in earnest. But I agree that a lot of consideration will have to be given to the way the words and phrases are configured. How our bodies intersect them. Arching text for example may be all wrong. A lot has to happen between this first crude sketch and its final iteration. In any case I want our interaction with his words to be performative.

Now to the question of how emotion seems guarded in my proposal. Wittgenstein's central point, it seems to me, is that the inexpressible can only be communicated by not direct-ly expressing it. It's in silence—in the non-saying—that it comes forward. (This all seems very Zen. Maybe I've been in California too long.) Somewhere W wrote—is it in his introduction or in one of his letters to Paul Engelmann or did I dream it?—that the Tractatus *is above all about ethics. But as far as I recall there are no direct propositions about ethics in it. So we have to assume that there is a high degree of metaphor in the* Tractatus. *My job then in constructing this plaza of language wouldn't be to make it more expres-sive, but would be to provide a space where his words can perform, and to do so in a style that is consistent with the restraint that he exhibits in his philosophical writings as well as in the austere house he designed for his sister. I have to curb my innate psychedelic instincts. Maybe I've entered my cold period. To quote R. Crumb's Mr. Natural, "Use the right tool for the job."*

DR: But you are making all this sound as unpsychedelic as possible.

Doug Hall: Yes, this project is not psychedelic at all.

DR: Wittgenstein psychedelic? Here I see...austerity. Because he would probably not believe this about art, that it is supposed to be philosophical. You don't get a sense that he is responsive to art that does the questioning.

Doug Hall: I don't think that in his time there was a vo-cabulary for that. There was no notion that art even could do that. I think that Duchamp was the person who turned art into a text. He demanded that we begin to examine the nature of the object itself.

2016, New York

I have been ruminating about this *Possibility* book for so long that I now have the opportunity to speak with Doug Hall again *twenty-one* years after I last interviewed him for this project. Talk about tenacity. His Wittgenstein Plaza was never built, but in 2016 he has a new Wittgenstein piece that soon will be installed:

Doug Hall: As the cliché of the dumbfounded museum visitor might say, "I don't know much about art but I know what I like." Well, I guess I could echo that by saying, I don't know much about Wittgenstein but I know what I like. When I was asked to propose an outdoor installation on the property of Steve Oliver, I began to imagine a sound installation with the text of the Tractatus *coming from the mouths of children. Over time as I began to think more deeply about it, I imagined the words spoken by young girls. I felt like this Germanic text needed the quality of their voices to bring out the meaning that I was convinced percolated in the silence just beneath the words. Walking around the property with Steve, we found a couple of groves of oaks and moss covered rocks that seemed appropriate and chose one that was quiet and protected. The speakers we're using are for the outdoors and can tolerate extreme weather conditions. And most importantly these incredible speakers are uncanny in the way they reproduce the human voice. They are mounted on stands and will be removed and stored during the winter rainy season. The sixteen speakers are arranged in three expanding rings. The four closest to the listening area are for the four soloists. Then there is a ring of six speakers that occupy a midrange. And finally an outer ring of six that are set far back among the distant trees. This arrangement allows us to mix the voices and manipulate them spatially so that the chorus can be heard in both mid- and far distance and from 360 degrees. The soloists are much closer in and feel more intimate, sometimes even speaking in whispers.*

DR: Is it a whole different thing when you are composing music?

Well, it's not really music, although it uses some musical structures like canons, among others. And not being a composer I had to construct the piece graphically in Photoshop, which I'm very comfortable with. My approach was similar to my process when making a video. I treated the statements like images and sort of storyboarded them in Photoshop.

Then I worked with Lisa Bielawa, a gifted and highly regarded composer and singer who was, until very recently, the artistic director of the San Francisco Girls Chorus. She along with Valerie Sainte-Agathe, the musical director and principle conductor, loved the project and helped me assemble a chorus of thirty-six choristers and four soloists from the younger ranks of the chorus school. Lisa took on the task of translating my graphic score into one that was notated and could be taught to the girls. With her in New York and me in San Francisco we skyped back and forth as she translated my crude score into a teachable musical language for the girls. Valerie rehearsed our chorus and got them ready to record at the sound stage at Skywalker Ranch.

One of the things I found so surprising about the Tractatus as I began to score it for a chorus of speaking voices is how rhythmic the phrases are. I don't know if this is because it was purposely written this way, it is a result of the translation, or it is just chance.

In any case there are rhythmic sections throughout that I wanted to amplify and take advantage of. I also scored the text so at times the language breaks down into abstraction and is no longer "saying" anything in any conventional way but is "showing" instead. Hard to know if Wittgenstein will be writhing in his grave, wishing he could cave in my head with a fire poker, or smiling with bemused pity. We recorded at Skywalker Sound on a beautiful spring day. One of the challenges we knew we would face is that because the girls are used to singing in a very precise way their interpretation of the score was going to be somewhat mechanical and stiff. Valerie worked with them to try and deal with this but there was a limit to what she could do in the time she had. So we recorded it much in the way I shoot video. With the understanding that the girls' sound images would be heavily edited and mixed in post. This became the job of the miraculous sound designers, Jim McKee and Jeremiah Moore, *who I've worked with for years on numerous projects. We all worked tirelessly to liberate the girls' voices so they would integrate with the surroundings on the ranch: the sound of the birds, the rustling of leaves, and most importantly reveal the beauty of Wittgenstein's words and ideas.*

DR: What did the girls think about the words they were singing?

They loved it! One of them said, "Well it sounds very important. It sounds very serious." The language is so evocative, especially when spoken by these children. One of the soloists, Hannah, was 8. I think the oldest member of the chorus was 12. They worked hard on it and of course Valerie, with a combination of respectable sternness and kindness, kept them focused.

DR: How do you feel about the romantic and the emotional in your work now that you are twenty years beyond your middle-aged "Cold Period" (when you were about the same age that I am now)?

Starts very softly. A soft whisper? And gets louder but never 'loud'. More like a m

Chorus A

— What cannnnn   beeee shown   cannot beeee   said What can be shown   ca
— can be shoooooown cannot be saiiiiidWhat can be shown   cannot be said   What can b
— be shooooown cannot be said   What can be shoooown cannot be said   What can be s
— cannot be said   What can be shown   cannot be said   What can be shown   cannot b

Chorus B

— What can be shoooown cannot be said   Whaaaaat can be shown cannot   be said
— be shown   cannot be said   What can be shoooooown cannot be saiiiiid   What ca
— cannnnn   beeee shown   cannot beeee   said What can be shown   cannot b
— shown   cannot be said What can be shown   cannot be said What can be shoooow

I think that one of the things that happens when you get older, or at least in my experience of aging, is that I care much less about how I'm being judged—including my often merciless self-judgments—which I suppose gives me a certain kind of emotional freedom. Perhaps I've entered what Edward Said and others have termed "late style." It's one of the benefits of aging. One of the few, I might warn you. Like everyone else, in the course of my life I've experienced a certain number of tragedies or heartbreaks, which have been both humbling and, I would like to believe, have made me just an itsy-bitsy more wise. We were lucky, privileged. We went to the best schools, we've been mentored by some of the best minds, and we thought we could do whatever we wanted to do, and in some sense we have, but we've also learned—or I have in any case—that the results are never going to be quite good enough. That's both the reward and the damnation of being an artist. And probably it's not a condition solely owned by artists.

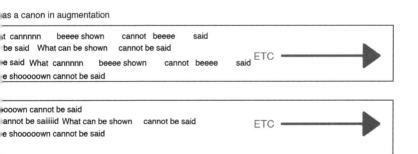

I think the Tractatus *is a deeply emotional work. A poetic masterpiece. It was written under harrowing circumstances during the First World War. Much of it sketched out in the trenches before he was taken prisoner of war by the French. Why is it that almost a hundred years after it was written we are still interested in it? I think it's because from what at first appears to be a disciplined treatise on the imperious logic of language there emerges a deeply felt apprehension that what matters to us—what really matters to us—is beyond the capability of language to express. This is an ageless observation. To my mind this begins to seep in most forcefully where he starts saying things like "Language disguises meaning" and "What can be shown cannot be said." I recall that this happens somewhere in the sections under the numeration 4. And this uncertainty, or lament as I like to call it, becomes more dominant in the closing sections of the book. This is what I hoped might come to the fore as one walked across his words etched into a plaza in Vienna or, probably a much better approach, listening to them spoken by children while sitting within a grove of trees on a ranch in Sonoma County, California. Beneath all this veneer of logic there is awareness of vulnerability and the inability of logic and language to address anything that really matters. Probably including philosophy itself.*

DR: "On what we cannot speak, we must remain silent"[103]— one of the best endings to any book. These aphorisms grab people! These single sentences with space around them. They have this *weight*. The same weight I felt when I heard the title of one of your earlier pieces, maybe a piece from that "Cold Period," *The Terrible Uncertainty of the Thing Described.*

Doug Hall: I am glad you remember that one. Thank you.

It was first shown in the 1980s. An exploration of ideas relating to the sublime. I was interested in how the language to describe the romantic landscape was like the same language used to describe the emergence of the Industrial Revolution. The equivalence between extreme forms of nature or extreme forms of industrial technology. The landscapes were all very turbulent—I videotaped on the Bering Sea, chased tornadoes for two seasons, filmed forest fires, then I went to Los Alamos and other locations where mechanical technologies mimicked, recreated or attempted to harness aspects of nature.... In the installation you see these highly refined projected images, four simultaneous tracks of video on those old-fashioned monitors and one projected, and in the room is a giant Tesla coil that periodically emits a huge jolt of electricity. You find yourself in this space looking at these images and not being quite sure where to stand, and then suddenly, for about 30 seconds you are confronted by an exploding bolt of lightning from the coil that arcs to two giant steel chairs enclosed behind a steel curtain that leans in toward the observer. And it is anything but cold. It is deeply emotional. How could a work that taps into the sublime be anything but?

DR: So what **is** the terrible uncertainty?

Doug Hall: I had a great answer at the time but I can't remember what it was.

I think it goes back to our earlier discussion. It is about our relationship to experiences that can't easily be catego-

rized, and our search for language to describe what can't be described. In our attempts to come up with descriptions, philosophers like Kant have given us concepts like the Sublime. Perhaps my love for the Tractatus *is that above all I experience it as literary sublime, which is just another way of saying I understand it as poetry.*

Doug Hall is now seventy-four years old, totally relaxed. His photographs sell for tidy sums in editions of six. He still does not trust words, or anyone who says they know what they mean.

Is Doug more *emotional* than two decades ago, when he was about the same age I am now? (I know *I* am more emotional. Hollywood films like *War Horse* now make me cry—they didn't used to. Back then maybe only Tarkovsky or Chris Marker would make me cry.)

Joseph Kosuth hooks on W's phrase "the meaning is the use." He wants art's meaning to come out in practice, while at the same time trying to change its purpose. He is now an elder statesman of conceptual art, art that makes a point through the ideas that structure it. My question is: Is the art form necessary to present the idea? Or does it merely obfuscate it, making things more confusing than they need to be? Writing about artworks should not cloud the immediacy of the works. They either grab us or they do not.

On a billboard, where you expect an advertisement, Kosuth places the following announcement:[104]

Is this blank? What we are accustomed to seeing here is part of the landscape. This text (sign, words) was made for this location, but it is a continuation of other things which may connect you to it. This sign (text, words) has a relationship with what you see around it. However, the ways in which it is different could constitute a criticism of the ways it is similar. Can this (text, sign) explain itself? And if it could would it mean what it says? This text, within a context of other signs, also wants to function as part of the 'real world', but it (as a text, as a sign) seems empty. The content that it shares with other signs is what connects you to this (sign, text, words); it is also what is missing.

A place where we expect an advertisement now offers us art: familiar medium, unfamiliar message. The text that is the analysis of itself. Is it a text? Is it a sign? Is everything a text, or a sign? Should art contain within itself its own explanation? Is this art's refuge when all else has been tried and found wanting?

The world is *not* a text: we comprehend the environment without words being plastered everywhere to tell us what we see. Yet if we close our eyes we can imagine what the view would be like if everything we see chose to advertise itself by explaining itself, and we might wonder whether we would wonder just what words were there to trust, and which were there to tear down.

"We don't *live* within any map, but still we continually try to use them. As it is with any picture of the world, it defines *as a picture* our relationship with the world."[105] No map is complete, no art can substitute for life. Then its meaning forgets its use. Kosuth's kind of art, and the kind of explanations he offers, play with concepts rather than elucidate them. As such it is a postmodern philosophy, calling up not so much quotations as *shards* from the past, the leftover shrapnel of ideas, far-flung pieces of understanding. W informs the possibility of connecting artworks to the explanations thrown at them. In his pithy ambiguity, he allows for the wonders of interpretation in the making of things altogether new.

There is a film about that unexpected dichotomy called *(Untitled)*, starring Adam Goldberg, directed by Jonathan Parker. Two brothers, one an artist, the other a composer, both interested in the same woman, a downtown gallerist. She says to the composer brother, "Your work isn't really music, but should be seen as sound art. Come perform it in my gallery, and maybe someone will purchase it as intangible art." Music is no luxury good that can be collected, while art is still a place the wealthy can spend their money on things that cannot be seen, just to show they can afford it. Only five people come to the composer's concert. Years later he meets one of them, who says, "That concert changed my life." Wittgenstein would approve.

"To say something is dead isn't to say that it's not around.... I've taken the precarious position of predicting that art will replace philosophy,"[106] says Kosuth. Philosophy has a lot to answer for, and art has many more games to play.

Doug Hall: The reason why Joseph Kosuth is important, and the reason why conceptualism is important, is that it attempts to address a problem in art by challenging Modernism's notion of "art for art's sake." It is a way for him, and a way for other artists, to address art as a philosophical problem, to ask questions about the nature of art itself, perhaps to question how we formulate meaning from it. Traditionally such questions have been largely the domain of aesthetics, which is a branch of philosophy.

But I think that the obvious problem, which Kosuth and others recognized, is that this approach ends up doing exactly what it is attempting to overcome, that is it ends up being totally self-referential, at the exclusion of the world, just the way I believe academic philosophy does. And so Kosuth's essay "The Artist as Anthropologist" was his attempt to address that very problem: how does the artist continue to function philosophically and yet reengage with the problems of the world?

DR: Yes, I have been reading Kosuth's book and trying to make sense of it, and several things about it still bother me. I cannot understand his logical flow, how he is picking quotes here and there and he is making these pronouncements, but they are neither beautiful nor making sense, they are just sort of antagonizing you.

I really don't understand the art, both in the book and the things I have seen. I don't get the sense of the craft of it—he is taking the easy way out. Just throwing the words on the wall—there it is! He is not turning it *into* something.

Doug Hall: I do not know. It depends on the pieces, and I have not seen all of them. I mean, it was only recently that I realized that the text pieces he is using, where words are being crossed out, are all based on Freud. I'm not sure why I missed that. I suppose because I didn't pay that much attention. I guess I was most taken by the physical presence of language and the problem of its being crossed out. Erased in a sense. Or repressed to reference Freud. When I actually saw the Freud piece at Castelli on Greene Street I responded to it as some kind of spatial experience, visually, and I found it striking and confounding. And I felt like this idea of words that are crossed out, their legibility erased, this idea of erasing or obscuring meaning somehow made sense to me.

And also, you have to understand that Kosuth's early work is so much a protest against the growing product orientation of the whole art world in the early 1970s and late 1960s. The conceptualism of Kosuth, Larry Weiner, and others was an attempt to move the visual arts away from romantic notions of the frenzied Expressionist into something that was perhaps more analytical, more philosophical. But what is odd—probably not odd but actually predictable—is how much his art came back to a kind of painterliness or at least austere beauty. And of course how naïve to imagine that anyone could intervene in art's march toward spectacular commercialism.

I do find the experience of his art phenomenologically gratifying. And I also think one's appreciation has to do with how you anticipate art functioning, how you interact with it, what your expectations are. And maybe it is enough to create a situation that is visually engaging, but also that is engaging in your brain.

DR: The title of my book is *The Possibility of Reddish Green*. That is a color which Wittgenstein didn't believe to exist. I think that you see it every autumn.

Doug Hall: That's interesting. If you use photographs, and you take a color temperature meter, you'll see red graying because there are filters for it. Fluorescent light creates a green cast in color film.

DR: So where does the reddish green appear?

Doug Hall: It appears where the green light of fluorescence and the warmer light of tungsten interact.

DR: That is a good example. This title suggests that there is something that cannot be said, cannot be seen, that we are looking for. So there is some sort of answer to the whole thing, looking for this way of thinking and constructing works of art and feeling things one step beyond.

Doug Hall: Well, that is the Sublime.

Leonardo da Vinci was fond of encouraging his students to carefully stare at the cracks in his studio's plaster walls. "Look long enough at those cracks," he smiled that famous smile. "You will see enough art and possibility there."

IX:

Lyric
Philosophy

Philosophy might be written as poetry, to be understood as a symphony might be heard. There are nonverbal, inexplicable ringings of truth, resonating with movements elsewhere, before and after thought. One wants to avoid the need for explanations; one wants to *feel* the truth. Canadian poet Jan Zwicky takes up this challenge.

Her book *Lyric Philosophy* is the ultimate schematic secondary text. On the left are her own words, written in fragments in the manner of W. On the right are quotations, from all across the world, words, music, pictures— the scrapbook behind the argument, the material from which we all may draw conclusions. For the symphony of thoughts, "look at the sentence as an instrument" (W). Listen to the structure of the book for the clue.[107]

Can we listen to philosophy, if from the page it does not speak? If it is not a script, but a record of questions? There is a philosophy of music but there should be a music of philosophy. Zwicky is cutting and pasting this together. It is a new way of looking at things. "The *Tractatus*," she writes, "is a sequence of variations on silence." (No wonder John Cage liked it.) On the corresponding righthand page is a page of a Schubert string quartet. A busy movement of sixty-fourth notes, easing out into a temporary conclusion. The music as written contains no rests.[108]

She also wrote a poetry book called *Wittgenstein Elegies*.

"To attend thoughtfully to resonance..."[109] A plea to hear truth in reverberation. An echo of the answer, though the attempt to explain goes nowhere. It's the feeling that there is more philosophy in the poem or the story than in the saber of logic. This is not to discredit the discipline, but only to remember completely what Novalis said: "Philosophy is a kind of homesickness, an urge to be at home everywhere." And nowhere. Having a good time, wish you were here.

You work out the system of explanation and it gets stronger, tougher, more complete with each new beam and girder. But then when finished it appears to have been built around a different object than the original question. That question has slipped away silently in the dark. It's laughing at you from behind a tree. You may glance up, surprise it, look straight in its eyes, and then you will know. Run straight to the woods.

Lyric Philosophy is a large-format coffee table scrapbook of philosophy. The book itself is beautiful, and should be displayed prominently. It's the size and shape of a midsize city's phonebook, but it invites gentle perusal as soon as it is opened.

> It is in this way, then, that philosophy might assume lyric form: when thought *whose eros is clarity* is driven also by profound intuitions of coherence—when it is also an attempt to arrive at an integrated perception, a picture or understanding of how something might affect us as beings with bodies and emotions as well as the ability to think logically.... When philosophy attempts to give voice to an ecology of experience.[110]

To explain how things connect, philosophy seeks strands of relation and relevance that have been overlooked. This is why the environment, or what surrounds us, is a philosophical matter, not only a scientific one. Which is being described in a new genre of literature, something that exists, but perhaps without a name. Where you read art looking for truth and logic looking for beauty, wondering which answer will make us cry. (Shall I cheapen it by naming it? Or is it easier to dissolve the borders with a turn of attention?)

Among the writers I have considered here, Jan Zwicky takes most seriously Wittgenstein's beguiling counsel: "philosophy ought really to be written only as a poetic composition."[111] What poetry did W have in mind? He does not refer specifically to poets as Heidegger so often does, but we know he liked Rilke and Trakl.

Perhaps this is because he was after an unwritten poetic, an approach to language still untried. We are trying it now, trying to make sense of the century, to survive the compression of language through the transformations of technology.

There is space, a blip on the screen, a gap, we turn away, the book is gone, the word crosses the page. Images fly by. I reach to connect them. There's too much booming and buzzing to hold fast to the plan. Everything could be worked into the narrative, every sudden connection could be explored for its poetic relevance.

Each fragment, a shard of paper, a comment, held together with huge paper clips. A student finds them, rummages through, lets the ideas loose, scatters them in the box like letters in the game of Scrabble, playing with concepts, reshuffling them. *Zettel.*[112] The box. Who wants to read this way? You have to, you must, there is no time for anything else. A poem may emerge, or it may not, or it may be a sequence of words unrecognizable, irreconcilable, irrespective of what is wanted. Sifting through the pieces, you learn that they do not fit together as if in a puzzle, but are linked as any two ideas may be linked—sensible only to those who are able to glimpse the paths between them.

Elizabeth Bishop imagined life in prison:

> I hope I am not being too reactionary when I say that my one desire is to be given one very dull book to read, the duller the better. A book, moreover, on a subject completely foreign to me.... From my detached rock-like book I shall be able to draw vast generalizations, abstractions of the grandest, most illuminating sort, like allegories or poems, and by posing fragments of it against the surroundings and conversations of my prison, I shall be able to form my own examples of surrealist art.[113]

Is this not an allegory of all reading?

To need words that "convey an awareness of their own inadequacy."[114] Not to be smug about the text, imagining the whole world as a book to be read. Only someone glazed by the alphabet would do that. The words on the page should never be all. They must point to the spaces they can never fill. They will be the scrawl that turns us away from language. Remain silent only to make communication possible, to sense the green immediacy of the world.

The word announces itself and holds its own, figure and also ground. Just as a truly interesting chord can be held out for hours as you begin to inhabit its tonal center, so the real word is not just a piece of syntax, but a mantra, a syllable encompassing itself, a milestone along the changing road of sound, like that unpronounceable Catalan *xarxa* twisting the tongue inscrutably for hours. They envelop themselves while revealing other paths. "Words," says my old teacher Seamus Heaney, "themselves are doors."[115]

The last bits of this book includes several memories from my education years ago. I am not sure my work discussed here is so significant, but I do find I cannot shake these memories, so it seems high time to write them down. All this questioning is getting to me.

Heaney had a way of taking anyone's writing and turning it into something that could be discussed and made alive for the class. This was a small writing seminar at Harvard University. Ten young scared poets, often afraid of the way their words came out. What the marks on the paper sounded like.

I for one was more terrified by this public revelation of my inner thoughts than just about anything else I was being asked to do. The poetry seemed so raw, so personal, so uncertain as to its own merit. It seemed to come both from the core of my very being and from some other place too far away, too flighty, too empty of the struggle to be worthy of consideration. These words, I found, just came out when the boom and buzz of experience seemed to alight upon a meaning. I did not know if they were poetic or not, but knew I wanted more than anything else to inhabit them once they were out there.

The door to the classroom was an entry to a sacred space, where these kinds of words were welcomed by the people gathered there. The group discussion of the poems was a door to the shared dream of the lyric, an enveloping of thought with the resonant, not reasoning, powers of sentence and phrase. I hoped these two could overlap, for that is what drove me into philosophy in the end. *And out again? Can the field contain what I now want to do? Can it tell me anything of how to proceed?*

I turned in one particular poem which I thought to be a genuine risk in the class of the master. In this work I cut out one-inch square pieces of maps from Norway and Nepal, and saw what the phrases written there, by chance, along with the shapes of the tracks and topographic contour lines, might suggest by way of of insight. This strange exercise seemed divorced from respect for the history of poetry and its solemnity, a history I never entirely felt comfortable within. Would my work be perceived as an insult? Weeks went by. I was afraid to ask Seamus what he thought.

Finally one day he came in, smiling with many xeroxed copies of "MAPS: PART ONE." Here are some pages of it now, early, unfinished, but another attempt at what we are still after, thirty-five long years later:

Guldebergodden

Y

There
a riverside stopped
by water,
Waiting for the other side
you entered the shallows
on foot
Circular waves surrounding
feet in the mud;

Rivers flow in a "Y"
branches reach for each other,
grasping into one
(Guldebergodden)
The current enters the lake
but disappears into
gentle windows
Above the winds light breakers
the giant "Y" surfaces
face down
Gazes beneath the waves.

Again
down a canyon
etch ed by the rain
drops Midtmaradalstindane
Barefoot on the sandy floor
pressed walls on which to lean
come ngain maradalsbreen
A diagonal cuts the smooth
tundra surface as a mistake
Ngan again
Ngan.

Memurubu
memory
murmurs ---- austere
Beware seracs in the white!
remembered
murmuring
'ruminations,
Runes, murals,
go east, east
ten down route
routed, rut$_d$
rutted
The whiteness re
members me
murmurumemu
rubumomeri
M
R
U

I smile as I insert these images, dug out of the attic, scanned and turned into the digital form that was far from existing when I wrote these words, remembering how excited I was to construct something in this way and how nervous I was when the great poet handed out copies to everyone in the class.

Part of me thinks these words are so much better than anything I am writing today because I believed so much in them and today I am hardly sure of anything. When I cut out those squares I set myself up for *a picture to hold me captive,* and drifted into the meanings that said picture, said map fragment, might wrench out of me.

Just a few years later I moved to Norway, traveled to some of those places, became no longer afraid of these long alien norsk words. *Bre* is a glacier, *tind* is a snowy summit, *midt* is the middle, *dal* is valley, so *Midtmaradalstindane* are the mountains in the middle of the Mara valley. So far *Mara* is just a name. A beautiful name.

The alien words become familiar in their lilting rolling strangeness like the irregular mountains of the arctic coasts, fairytale shapes no one thinks can actually exist but of course they are there.

Wittgenstein himself bought a *hytte* not far from these very mountains, a cabin in Norway where he could think and live in total peace. Over the years his ability in the Norwegian language rose and fell, just as I find my own doing as I only occasionally return to this fabulous landscape and its beautiful words, mountains, and people.

Did he also mouth out the words on street and shop signs and wonder to himself, "Why is it that I can speak this language?"

Seamus Heaney was certainly one of the greatest teachers I was privileged to study with, because he always knew how to take any writing that was submitted to our writing workshop and say just the right thing about it to the assembled hopeful. And did he think I was a poet? "You're on the edges." On the edges I remain.

My picture-poems were far away from the serious lyricism that my fellow students turned in. Many of them became successful poets, possibly because of this class. I feel so lucky to have been there, since I had absolutely no idea what I was doing and probably still don't.

"Lyric art," says Zwicky, "is the fullest expression of the hunger for wordlessness."[116] (At least the fullest expression *using* words.) If you pay close attention to what surrounds you there is little need for the dusty catalogs of memory. At any one moment, at any place, around any of us, there is so much going on. Words delve into the dictionary of experience, and imagine it all can be named. The name, like the machine, should never forget what it is not. What it can't see. What it blinds us from seeing. "[W]ords are bent to the shape of wordlessness. (The tension of the bow which gives thought the power to move.)"[117]

To be enveloped by the world, to find complete oneness within it, that's an idea, a poetic goal: a loss of the self in the singularity of the embracing earth. You sense it but you cannot live there. It is touched on in instances, moments of dissolving reflection. This is why poems often need only to be several lines in length. Poetic philosophy needs to find its own essential form. This form will embrace question and answer, explanation and hint, rhetoric and logic, and fill a hollow within us that each of these polar opposites on its own cannot fulfill.

Logic will learn to blend impossible colors. Literature will not be afraid of investigating its own insights.

The last time I saw Seamus Heaney was in Dublin, after he came to a talk I gave on my book *Survival of the Beautiful* at the Science Gallery, a most unusual museum that blends the empirical and the artistic. I talked about how evolution was always considered by Darwin to include the unfurling and development of beauty, in appearance, act, and process, in those endless animal forms appearing over the millions of years that have led up to this instant. It wasn't poetry but I did play some music, showing what the music of the nightingale has in common with the song of the whale. I don't know if we were listening-to or listening-as, to imagine something Wittgenstein might say. Seamus was always gracious whenever I sent him things, and he told me he had gotten through some rough years but was seeing everything in a more positive light. I am sorry I did not see him more often.

In the new century, the bow and the lyre become the laser and the bell.[118] The tools that can be metaphors for the cosmos change, but the use of instruments to catch hold of the divine continues. The burning light of reason reflects in the peal of the song. Cutting through oneness, you may race by *or* resound with the quaking leaves. Bertrand Russell remembered this:

> W used to come to see me every evening at midnight, and pace up and down my room like a wild beast for three hours in agitated silence. Once I said to him: "Are you thinking about logic or about your sins?" "Both," he replied, and continued his pacing.[119]

I meet Jan Zwicky trying to defend lyric philosophy in front of a possibly hostile audience in a city of the western prairies. Wind in the trees out the window, cottonwood fluff blowing into the grass, thunderstorms rumbling each afternoon. She paces above the fragmentary writings of Heraclitus, lamenting his neglect, defending her presentation and her choice of method. I think: Why try to explain something that only makes sense in the doing? The lyric needs to be evoked, not cautioned into being. We can take it. As always, there should be no apologies. We do what we do. We think the way we must, and structure our ideas in the only honest way we believe they can be organized. There need be no excuses, if the revolution in thought will let us dance.

People are behind all these words—this may be something W never understood. He followed abstraction far more than story. He might not be amused by the idea of a novel in which he appears.

We who read too much, all we can do honestly is quote from our paper worlds. These papers yellow and decay. The tin box of memory holds only fragments, you know. And the paper clips that clasp them *rust*.

We who read too little, who remember even less, have to hope for fragments that will stand the test of time, small slivers that will last longer than their contexts and the memory of those that who said them.

The rust shows the ephemerality of organization. The pieces will remain to be re-sorted long after the explanation has rendered itself obsolete. The material of history, too, disintegrates. After a long while it will only be the past interpretations that will be decipherable, held together by new and constantly changing ways of drawing order out of chaos.

thought clearly. Everything that can be said can be said clearly.

4.12 Propositions can represent the whole reality, but they cannot represent what they must have in common with reality in order to be able to represent it—the logical form.

To be able to represent the logical form, we should have to be able to put ourselves with the propositions outside logic, that is outside the world.

4.121 Propositions cannot represent the logical form : this mirrors itself in the propositions.

That which mirrors itself in language, language cannot represent.

That which expresses *itself* in language, *we* cannot express by language.

The propositions *show* the logical form of reality.

They exhibit it.

4.1211 Thus a proposition "*fa*" shows that in its sense the object *a* occurs, two propositions "*fa*" and "*ga*" that they are both about the same object.

If two propositions contradict one another, this is shown by their structure ; similarly if one follows from another, etc.

4.1212 What *can* be shown *cannot* be said.

4.1213 Now we understand our feeling that we are in possession of the right logical conception, if only all is right in our symbolism.

4.122 We can speak in a certain sense of formal properties of objects and atomic facts, or of properties of the structure of facts, and in the same sense of formal relations and relations of structures.

(Instead of property of the structure I also say

Credo

Philosophy wants to explain it all, but its questions are there for the taking. We read it, absorb what we want, and then ignore the rest. All these writers and artists have done it. I do the same. As Kierkegaard said, no system is ever worth its claim to completion. For these are forays into what cannot be completely articulated. The artistic vision grasps for a moment of truth by example, by insight, while the philosophical wants to explain. And yet when it works, it too is a kind of art: beautiful arguments, images limned in logic upon which to reflect.

I have often found more philosophical insights in art than in argument, so my bias is clear. Still, just as there is philosophical art and less philosophical art, so there is artistic philosophy and a more mundane kind as well.

Doubt, doubt continues and even motivates the path of the inquiry. Aphorisms, independent phrases, are they especially easy for our time, or have they always been an option? Heraclitus, for example, makes more sense to us today as fragments than he might make were we to obtain more complete records of what he wrote.

Heraclitus tried desperately to use piecemeal words to evoke the smooth and the flexible. The paradoxes that troubled him are normal to us now, as the essential movement of our world is today understood only as a series of snapshots of frozen time. Real rivers are too easy to bypass these days with the tunnel or the bridge. Even the ferry boatman, who winks to let on that he realizes you know who he really is, has nearly become a thing of the ineffable past. Let no natural impasse stand in our paths—we, who have built so many ways to travel from place to place ignoring what comes along the way. Living in a way hell-bent on making the future as different from the past as it possibly can be, what use is there making any guesses on where it might go. "We are *or* are not."

It may not be the aphorism, but the space between the words that matters most. Space in which to think, to fill in the blanks with your own thoughts.

Anger at the lost nature of the language of prediction, the cold waters carrying us downstream to the plummeting falls. Down the cascades to frothy white mist, splintering on the rocks, broken to pieces at last. A world made of many rivers, each of us living in the current and crossing to opposite banks. No unity to the message, just the incontestable ambiguity of all those most important parts of it. Sail down your dissipating streams. Step at once in the many tributaries feeding the one great ocean. It has no farther shore, and no end.

To take in one thought at a time, what more could be expected of us amidst a relentless swirl of ideas? It is a prerequisite to leave space around each thought to ready us to take it in. This may not be the best way for things to be, but it is as they seem.

Are the above examples of interpretations of Wittgenstein, or of philosophy, mere curiosities? The significance of a philosophy is measured by the *range* of its interpretations, the depth to which it penetrates culture. W has touched many, far and wide. They are genuinely caught up in his life and his insights. We all have our different tools which we can apply to the problem. Toward the end of his life he told Drury this:

> "Yes, I have reached a real resting-place. I know that my method is right. My father was a business man, and I am a business man: I want my philosophy to be businesslike, to get something done, to get something settled."[120]

W sets a standard, then he sets a mood. These almost seem to oppose each other, the refusal to compromise, and an openness to the poetic simile as the answer to a question: it's like clearing the air only to fill it with clouds.

> "Philosophy is like trying to open a safe with a combination lock: each little adjustment of the dials seems to achieve nothing; only when everything is in place does the door open."[121]

How philosophy *lives* through such interpretations. How the answers to its questions often fall outside its boundaries. You go to philosophy to ask. You go elsewhere to answer.

In one of my first seminars in graduate school we had a particularly tough young professor. This may have been her first job in front of a classroom. I walked in one day while she was eviscerating one of my fellow students with great ferocity. "Listen to these lines in this so-called 'paper' of yours," she glared. "These aren't arguments, this is rubbish." My classmate appeared gutted like a fish. Tears were welling up in his eyes. My god, I thought, is this what a class with Wittgenstein was like? Is this how severe philosophy is meant to be? This was still the beginning of the semester! This new professor was younger than most of us students and she seemed ready to bring us all down. I would be next. I grumbled inside, and readied myself for the attack.

"*Mr.* Rothenberg, just what do you think you are up to here in this pathetic excuse for an assignment? How dare you suggest such hokum about the rabbit and the duck?"

I had turned in an analysis of the famous rabbit-duck diagram, which originally appeared in the German humor magazine *Fliegende Blätter* in 1892, was noted by American psychologist Joseph Jastrow in 1899, but was made essential for philosophers by Ludwig Wittgenstein in the *Investigations*:[122]

You've all seen this famous friendly face. I had always been told it had to be one or the other, that our minds are engaged in 'seeing-as' and we will see either a rabbit or a duck, never both at the same time.

I had been reading an article by phenomenologist Don Ihde, who urged us to be cautious with such trained absolutes. Come on, he argued, it is neither rabbit not duck, just lines on a page.[123] Cross-hatching, shading, outlines, illusions. Go for the thing itself, not what someone tells you it is supposed to mean.

"Rothenberg, that is complete nonsense and you know it. You are insulting the whole profession of philosophy."

"Not necessarily, professor, I am simply reporting another philosopher's view on the situation."

"A very misguided view to be sure."

"You might think so, but I think it deserves our consideration. These lines on the page, these markings or these words, can always mean more than any one interpretation. If we can't see the rabbit and duck at once, we see nothing. We miss that the point can be perceived, not only thought."

I was not going to let her get the better of me this time. I wasn't sure of anything, but I didn't think philosophy class was the right place for insult and humiliation.

"I can't stand your insolence, Rothenberg," our young professor shouted. *"It's as if you are treating me as an EQUAL!"*

"That's exactly how you should treat us, professor."

And I hope you feel, readers, that that is how you have been treated in this aphoristic journey through the ways philosophy can vex and inspire people from various walks of art, literature, and life.

Wabbit season. Duck season. Wabbit season. Duck season. This version of the picture is more friendly:

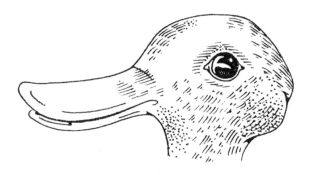

"And you, what do you seek?" was to be the final chapter of surrealist mountaineer René Daumal's exemplary novel of spiritual quest, *Mount Analogue*.[124] He died before writing it, and how could he have lived, with that perplexity on his lips? Only you know what you are meant to seek. Only you know how a piece of another's lifework can inspire. Only you know your possible route through open space, through a field blazing in a color no one else even thinks can exist, across the valley to the mountains beyond, rising so far into the clouds that everyone has told you they are mythical, beyond the reach of human proportion.

Time to close the book and discover why. All your colors are out there, flying.

I had already studied mathematics, a mad kind of horizontal reasoning like a landscape that exists entirely on its own, when it is more natural to lie in the grass and make love, glistening, the whole length of the river. Because small, noisy waves, as from strenuous walking, pounded in my ears, I stopped my bleak Saturday, while a great many dry leaves dropped from the sycamore.

This possibility must have been in color from the beginning.

—Rosmarie Waldrop, *The Reproduction of Profiles*[125]

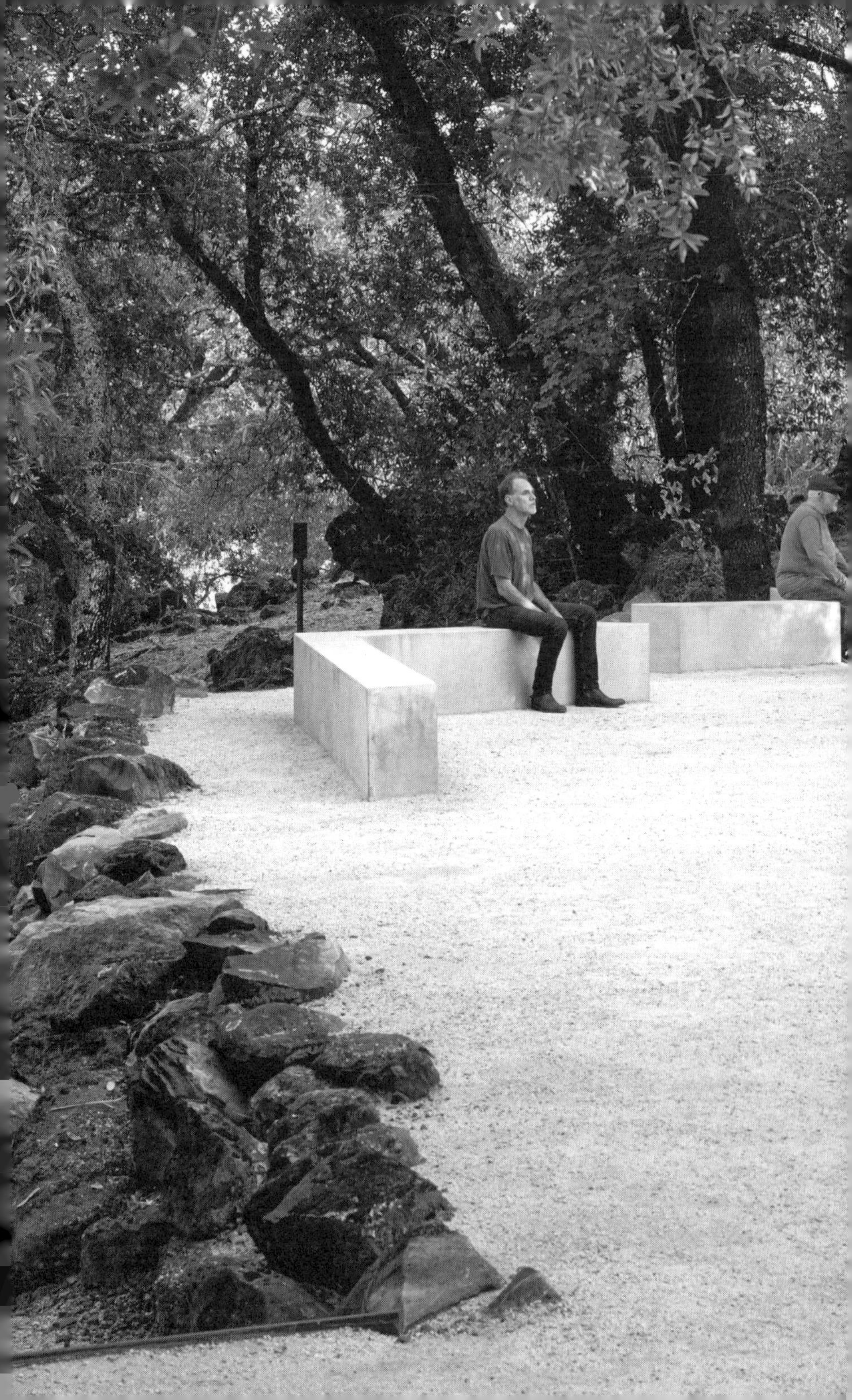

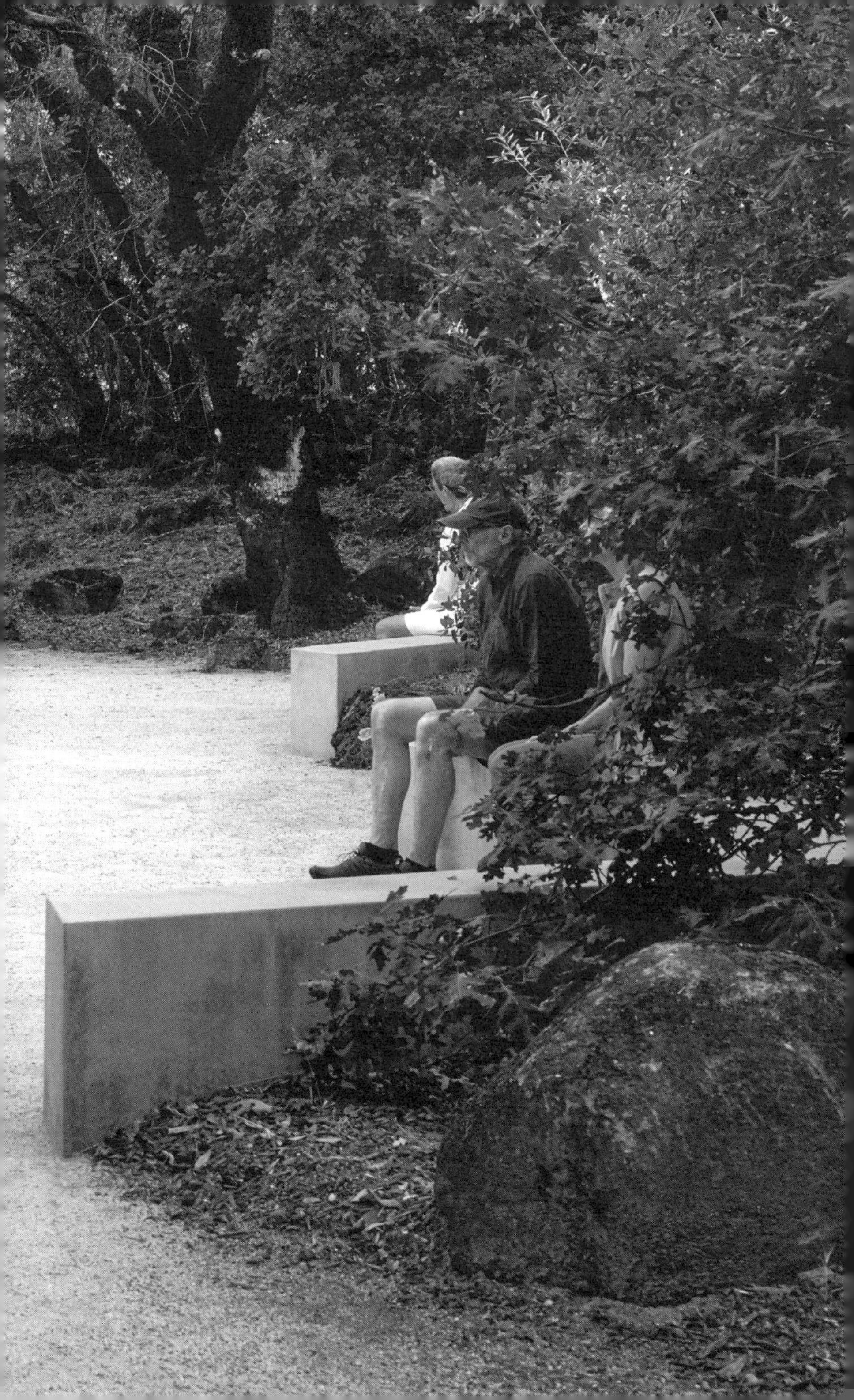

Notes

1 Wallace Stevens, "Like Decorations in a Nigger Cemetary," in *Collected Poems* (New York: Vintage, 1982), p. 161.
2 Ludwig Wittgenstein, *Culture and Value* (Oxford: Blackwell, 1998), p. 48.
3 Ibid, p. 70.
4 Ludwig Wittgenstein, *Notebooks 1914-1916*, ed. G.H. von Wright and G.E.M. Anscombe (New York: Harper, 1961), August 12th, 1916, p. 80e.
5 *Notebooks*, August 13th, 1916, p. 81e.
6 Ludwig Wittgenstein, *Philosophical Investigations*, trans. G. E. M. Anscombe, P. M. S. Hacker and Joachim Schulte, revised 4th edition (Malden: Blackwell, 2009), 34, p. 20.
7 *Investigations*, 57, p. 32.
8 *Investigations*, 78, p. 41.
9 *Investigations*, 115, p. 53.
10 *Investigations*, 172, p. 76.
11 *Investigations*, 219, p. 92.
12 *Investigations*, 535, p. 152.
13 See David Rothenberg, *Sudden Music* (Athens: University of Georgia Press, 2000), pp. 4-10. And *The Way of Pure Sound: An Inquiry into the Music of the Gyaling*, which can be downloaded here: https://tinyurl.com/thhjsv9
14 *Investigations*, 610, p. 167.
15 Ibid.
16 *Investigations*, 691, p. 180.
17 Today this section of the *Investigations* is no longer known as "Part II," but instead called *Philosophy of Psychology: A Fragment.*
18 *Investigations*, Philosophy of Psychology, 1, p. 181.
19 *Investigations*, Philosophy of Psychology, 35, p. 190.
20 *Investigations*, Philosophy of Psychology, 40, p. 191.
21 There is one letter from John Cage to me in the recently published *Letters of John Cage* (Middletown: Wesleyan University Press, 2016), but not this one. I think it was from a conversation we had in 1988.
22 *Investigations*, Philosophy of Psychology, 55, p. 193.
23 *Investigations*, Philosophy of Psychology, 143, p. 208.
24 Philip Kerr, *A Philosophical Investigation* (New York: Farrar, Straus, Giroux, 1993), p. 2.
25 Ibid, p. 217.
26 Ibid, p. 242.
27 Ibid, p. 170.
28 Ibid, pp. 298-299.
29 Ray Monk, *Wittgenstein: The Duty of Genius* (New York: Penguin, 1991), p. 187.
30 Philip Kerr, *A Philosophical Investigation*, p. 330.
31 Ibid, p. 363.
32 Terry Eagleton, *Saints and Scholars* (London: Verso, 1987), p. 144.
33 Derek Jarman, *Wittgenstein: A Film* (Bloomington: Indiana University Press, 1992), p. 66.
34 Ibid, p. 108 [originally from Norman Malcolm's book *Wittgenstein: A Memoir*].
35 Ray Monk, *Wittgenstein: The Duty of Genius*, p. 498.
36 Ibid, pp. 373-374.
37 Ibid, p. 376.

38   Ibid, p. 377.
39   Ibid, p. 504.
40   Ibid, p. 505.
41   Benjamin Franklin, *The Autobiography of Benjamin Franklin* (Philadelphia: Henry Altemus, 1895 [1788]), pp. 147-148.
42   Jarman, *Wittgenstein: A Film*, p. 124.
43   Ibid, p. 142.
44   Mark Anderson, Afterword to Thomas Bernhard, *The Loser*, trans. Jack Dawson (New York: Knopf, 1991), p. 173.
45   Thomas Bernhard, *Witttgenstein's Nephew*, trans. David McLintock (New York: Knopf, 1989), p. 23.
46   Ibid, p. 81.
47   Ibid, p. 25.
48   Ibid, pp. 62-63.
49   Thomas Bernhard, *Correction*, trans. Sophie Wilkins (New York: Knopf, 1979), p. 107.
50   Thomas Bernhard, *Wittgenstein's Nephew*, pp. 81-82.
51   Thomas Bernhard, *Correction*, p. 8.
52   Ibid, p. 11.
53   Paul Wijdeveld, *Ludwig Wittgenstein: Architect* (London: Thames and Hudson, 1994), p. 45.
54   Ludwig Wittgenstein, *Culture and Value*, p. 16.
55   Thomas Bernhard, *Correction*, p. 42.
56   Ibid, p. 18.
57   Ibid, pp. 162-163.
58   Thomas Bernhard, *Wittgenstein's Nephew*, p. 53.
59   Ibid, p. 160.
60   Italo Calvino, *The Road to San Giovanni*, trans. Tim Parks (New York: Pantheon, 1993), pp. 32-33.
61   Maurice Drury, *The Danger of Words* (London: Bloomsbury, 1973), p. 107.
62   Thomas Bernhard, *Correction*, p. 1.
63   Ibid, p. 271.
64   Paul Wijdeveld, *Ludwig Wittgenstein: Architect*, p. 42.
65   Maurice Drury, *The Danger of Words*, p. 120.
66   Max Frisch, *Man in the Holocene*, trans. Geoffrey Skelton (New York: Harcourt Brace Jovanovich, 1979), p. 6.
67   Chris Marker, *La Jetée: Cine-Roman* (New York: Zone Books, 1992), p. 82.
68   David Markson, *Wittgenstein's Mistress* (Champaign: Dalkey Archive, 1988), p. 12.
69   Ibid, p. 65.
70   Ibid, p. 79.
71   Ibid, p. 100.
72   Ibid, p. 170.
73   Ibid, p. 171.
74   Ibid, pp. 231-232.
75   Ray Monk, *Wittgenstein: The Duty of Genius*, p. 579.
76   David Markson, *Wittgenstein's Mistress*, p. 232.
77   Ibid, p. 240.

78 Ludwig Wittgenstein, *Remarks on Colour*, ed. G.E.M. Anscombe, trans. Linda McAlister and Margarete Schättle (Berkeley: University of California Press, 1977), I, 15, p. 4. References throughout this chapter follow the convention of numbered paragraphs in the original.

79 Johann Wolfgang von Goethe, *Theory of Colours*, trans. Charles Eastlake (London: John Murray, 1840). References throughout this chapter follow the convention of numbered paragraphs in the original.

80 Johann Wolfgang von Goethe, *Theory of Colours*, 751, p. 300.

81 Ludwig Wittgenstein, *Remarks on Colour*, II, 3, p. 15.

82 Goethe, *Theory of Colours*, 753-754, p. 301-302.

83 Wittgenstein, *Remarks on Colour*, III, 43, p. 23 and III, 303, p. 57.

84 Goethe, *Theory of Colours*, 52, p. 22.

85 Wittgenstein, *Remarks on Colour*, III, 117, p. 30.

86 "How to see reddish-green," *New Scientist*, vol. 100, p. 178, Oct. 20, 1983.

87 Goethe, *Theory of Colours*, 739, pp. 293-294.

88 See W.I. Homer, *Seurat and the Science of Painting* (Cambridge: MIT Press, 1964), p 164ff. Or C.L. Hardin, *Color for Philosophers* (Boston: Hackett, 1991), p. 102.

89 Goethe, *Theory of Colours*, 38, p. 15.

90 Wittgenstein, *Remarks on Colour*, I, 71-72, p. 12.

91 Jonathan Westphal, "Whiteness," in *Goethe and the Sciences: A Reappraisal* (Dordrecht: D. Reidel, 1987), p. 328.

92 Klaus Meyer-Abich, "Self-Knowledge, Freedom, and Irony: The Language of Nature in Goethe," in *Goethe and the Sciences: A Reappraisal* (Dordrecht: D. Reidel), 1987, p. 362.

93 Wittgenstein, *Remarks on Colour*, I, 53, p. 9.

94 Goethe, *Theory of Colours*, 716, p. 283.

95 Ibid, 718, p. 284.

96 Wittgenstein, *Remarks on Colour*, III, 317, p. 58.

97 Ibid, III, 317, p. 58.

98 Quoted by Carl Friedrich von Weizsacker in *Goethe and the Sciences,* ed. Frederick Amrine et al (Dordrecht: Reidel, 1987), p. 130.

99 Marjorie Perloff, *Wittgenstein's Ladder: Poetic Language and the Strangeness of the Ordinary* (Chicago: University of Chicago Press, 1996), p. 221.

100 Joseph Kosuth, *Art After Philosophy and After* (Cambridge: MIT Press, 1991), p. 14.

101 Ibid, p. 35.

102 First conversation with Doug Hall, San Francisco, February, 1995. Second conversation with Doug Hall, New York, September 2016. [I have been working on this book a long time.]

103 Literally "Whereof one cannot speak, thereof one must be silent," Ludwig Wittgenstein, *Tractatus Logico-Philosophicus* (London: Kegan Paul, 1922), p. 7.

104 Joseph Kosuth, *Text/Context*, Edinburgh 1979. Plate 25 in Kosuth, *Art After Philosophy and After*.

105 Ibid, p. 235.

106 Joseph Kosuth, "Footnote to Poetry," in *Art After Philosophy and After*, p. 35.

107 Jan Zwicky, *Lyric Philosophy* (Toronto: University of Toronto Press, 1992), p. 49.

108 Ibid, p. 52.

109 Ibid, p. 78.

110 Ibid, p. 124.

111 Ibid, p. 176.
112 Ludwig Wittgenstein, *Zettel*, ed. G.E.M Anscombe and G.H. von Wright (Berkeley: University of California Press, 2007).
113 Jan Zwicky, *Lyric Philosophy*, p. 195.
114 Ibid, p. 202.
115 Ibid, p. 203.
116 Ibid, p. 246.
117 Ibid, p. 256.
118 Ibid, p. 318.
119 Ibid, p. 385.
120 Maurice Drury, *The Danger of Words*, p. 110.
121 Ibid, p. 111.
122 *Investigations*, Philosophy of Psychology, 118, p. 204.
123 Don Ihde, "Wittgenstein's Phenomenological Reduction," in *Sense and Significance* (Pittsburgh: Duquesne University Press, 1973), p. 156.
124 René Daumal, *Mount Analogue*, trans. Roger Shattuck (San Francisco: City Lights, 1971).
125 Rosmarie Waldrop, "The Reproduction of Profiles," in *Curves to the Apple* (New York: New Directions, 2006), p. 6.

Illustration Credits

47, 119, 172   Pages from the notebooks of Muriel Wood-Ponzecchi's copy of Wittgenstein's *Tractatus*. Muriel Wood-Gerlach (later Ponzecchi) received her PhD in Behavioral Sciences in Applied Mathematics and Statistics at Stanford University in 1957 and taught Philosophy at UC Santa Barbara and The American College in Paris.

75-78   Photos and plans of the house Wittgenstein designed in Vienna, from Paul Wijdeveld, *Ludwig Wittgenstein: Architect* (London: Thames and Hudson, 1994).

89-103   Drawings of Ludwig Wittgenstein by Swedish artist Leif Haglund, who works since 1980 with traditional and digital tools: fine art, video, installations, performance, web applications. Humankind and our relationship to nature and society makes up the main content of his images.

140, 141   Doug Hall, *Wittgenstein Plaza* (proposal, 1992). Doug Hall is an internationally known artist who has worked for over forty years in a wide range of media, including performance, installation, video, and large format photography. His works are collected by major museums all over the world. He is professor emeritus at The San Francisco Art Institute, where he taught from 1980 until 2008.

147-149   Doug Hall, *Wittgenstein Garden* (2016); selections from the score.

153   Joseph Kosuth, *Text/Context: Edinburgh 1979*. Plate 25 in Joseph Kosuth, *Art After Philosophy and After* (Cambridge: MIT Press, 1991).

178, 180   Duck/rabbit diagram, https://en.wikipedia.org/wiki/Rabbit%E2%80%93duck_illusion

182-183   Doug Hall, *Wittgenstein Garden* (2016), photograph of the work by Jeremiah Moore, 2018.

David Rothenberg is distinguished professor of philosophy and music at the New Jersey Institute of Technology. He is a noted writer on themes connecting humanity, nature, and technology and music. He is the author of *Why Birds Sing* (Basic Books and Penguin UK, 2005), *Hand's End: Technology and the Limits of Nature* (California, 1993), *Thousand Mile Song* (Basic Books, 2008), *Survival of the Beautiful* (Bloomsbury, 2011), *Bug Music* (St. Martins, 2013) and *Nightingales in Berlin* (Chicago, 2019 and Rowohlt, 2020).

As a musician Rothenberg has recorded for the ECM, Gruenrekorder, and Clermont labels. Among his many recordings are *One Dark Night I Left My Silent House*, with Marilyn Crispell, and *Cicada Dream Band*, with Pauline Oliveros. He has performed or recorded with Peter Gabriel, Scanner, Suzanne Vega, Iva Bittova, Pete Seeger, Mamadou Kelly and Jaron Lanier, among many others, playing clarinets and various electronic and natural sounds.

www.davidrothenberg.net